MW01097872

Prof. Panayotis Papazoglou, PhD

The Ultimate Educational Guide to MIPS Assembly Programming

First English edition (translation from Greek): 2018
Kessariani, Athens, Greece
email: **p.m.papazoglou@hotmail.com**

book figures: **Panayotis Papazoglou**

ISBN-13: 978-1727880878

ISBN-10: 1727880870

Follow your dreams!

PREFACE

The MIPS microprocessor is the most known represeter of the RISC design philosophy and constitutes an ideal tool for introducing Assembly programming. Moreover, the MIPS 32bit Assembly is the most popular tool among Universities due to simplicity for learning and understanding.

This book has been written from a pure educational point of view and constitutes an ideal learning tool for students.

Additionally, this book has some unique features such as:

- understandable text
- flow charts analysis
- step by step code development
- well documented code
- analytic figures
- laboratory exercises

It is important to note that the whole book material has been tested under real conditions in higher education. By buying this book you have access to download material such as lab solution manual and power point presentations.

This book constitutes the ultimate educational guide which offers important knowledge and demystifies the Assembly programming. Moreover, this book has been written by taking in account the real needs of students, teachers and others who want to develop MIPS Assembly based applications.

The above lines, state the deep belief of the author that this book will constitute a great teaching and educational tool for helping anyone understand the MIPS 32bit Assembly language. On the other hand, the book can be easily used by the teacher for organizing lectures and presentations as well as the laboratory exercises.

Prof. Panayotis Papazoglou, PhD

The book structure

The book consists of 5 chapters.

The first steps in Assembly programming are presented in the **first chapter** as well as the basic features and instructions of the MIPS 32bit microprocessor.

In **second chapter** the first applications using instructions, functions and programming structures will be developed. A main goal is to show that every program is based mainly on the available system functions.

The filling, reading and processing of array data are basic procedures that are presented in **third chapter**. The goal is to present the array management methods in the physical memory and to understand the corresponding addressing modes.

In **fourth chapter**, lab exercises organized in steps are presented. This exercises are well structured for helping the students to work autonomously and to learn how to think.

In **fifth chapter**, the basic MIPS Assembly instructions are presented as well as an instruction list with the corresponding description.

Finally, a short guide for using the MIPS (SPIM/QtSPIM) simulator is presented.

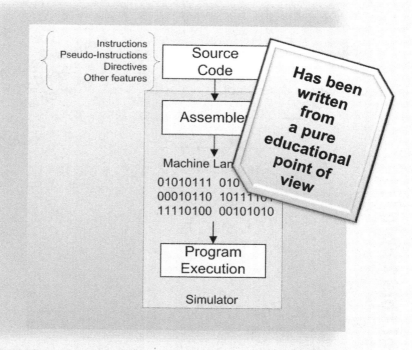

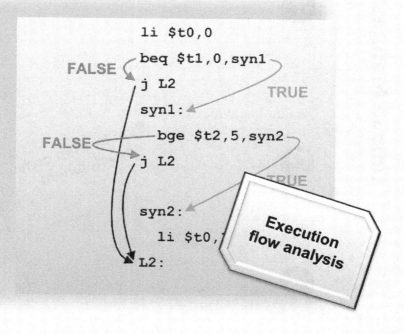

Unique features of this book!

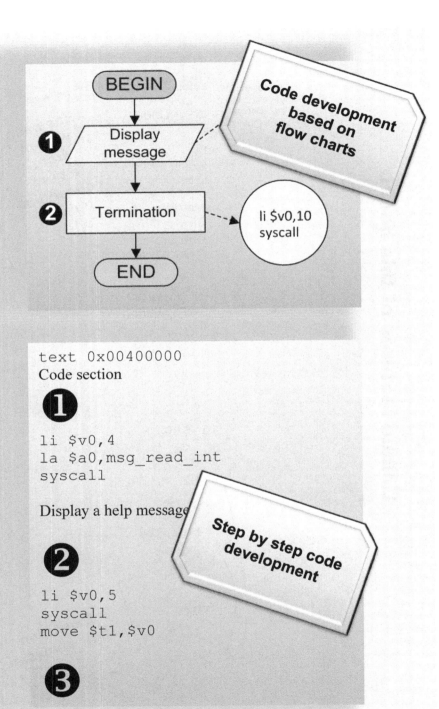

BEGIN

❶ Display message

Code development based on flow charts

❷ Termination

li $v0,10
syscall

END

```
text 0x00400000
```
Code section

❶

```
li $v0,4
la $a0,msg_read_int
syscall
```

Display a help message

❷

Step by step code development

```
li $v0,5
syscall
move $t1,$v0
```

❸

1 Introduction to the MIPS 32bit Microprocessor Programming

Content-Goals

The MIPS microprocessor is the most known representer of the RISC design philosophy and constitutes an ideal tool for introducing Assembly programming. The first steps in Assembly programming will be presented in this chapter as well as the basic features and instructions of the MIPS 32bit microprocessor.

Chapter Contents

1.1 Introduction
1.2 Registers
1.3 Memory model
1.4 MIPS Programming

1.1 Introduction

In this chapter, the basic features of the MIPS 32 bit microprocessor as well as basic concepts and Assembly programming will be presented. The chapter presentation is focused on the needed features that are critical for the programmer in order to develop operational code.

For testing the source code and due to the fact that the most computer systems (office, home, university) are not based on a MIPS microprocessor, a MIPS simulator will be used. Moreover, the programs in the next chapters are limited by the simulator features. Thus, program deviations exist from a real MIPS microprocessor programming. The simulation software that will be used is free and can be downloaded from the internet. **A quick guide for developing and executing MIPS programs inside the simulator environment is presented in appendix A.**

1.2 Registers

The MIPS microprocessor has 32 general purpose registers, two special purpose for arithmetic operations and a program counter. Every register corresponds to a unique number (identifier) and inside programs is used with its symbolic name. For simplicity reasons, only the symbolic names are used. Figure 1.1 shows the available registers for the MIPS microprocessor.

what is a register?

Think a register as a variable which is implemented with a specific digital circuit inside the microprocessor. Each microprocessor has its own registers, with specific names and capacity. For developing an Assembly program and for exchanging data with the microprocessor, the available registers are used.

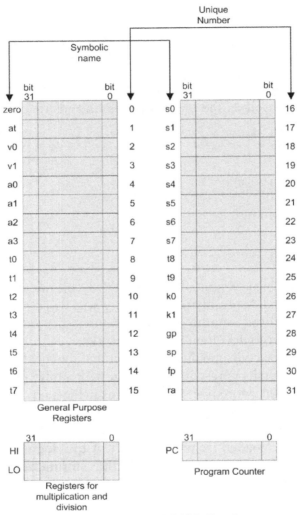

Figure 1.1 MIPS 32bit Registers

For using registers 0 to 31, the corresponding unique number or symbolic name can be used. Practically, all the programmers prefer the symbolic names. Moreover, inside programs the prefix '$' is used on the left of a register number or symbolic name. As an example, the register v0 can be used by writing $v0 or $2.

1.3 Memory model

MIPS uses a classical memory model that can be used by the programmer. The upper memory address is 7FFFFFFFh (letter 'h' denotes a hexadecimal number). The memory is organized in areas as follows:

(a) code area (text) which hosts the program instructions
(b) data area (data) which hosts the data that are processed by programs
(c) stack area (stack)

Figure 1.2 shows the memory organization with the corresponding areas and addresses.

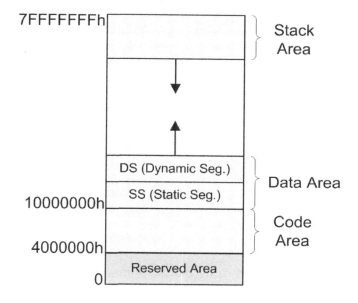

Figure 1.2 MIPS memory model

As shown in figure 1.2, the Data Area consists of two segments, one dynamic (DS) and one static (SS). The static segment (SS) has specific address limits. When a larger amount of data will be stored, more memory locations are needed as compared to the available locations of the static segment. Thus, more locations are occupied towards the higher addresses. Additionally, over the data area, the stack area is placed. The memory locations occupation towards the higher address can causes a collision with the stack contents. For solving that issue, the stack direction is to lower addresses starting from the higher address. Thus, the possibility of a data collision is extremely low.

1.4 MIPS Programming

For Assembly program execution, an "interpretation" in machine language is required. This requirement is fulfilled by the Assembler which is somehow equivalent to a compiler that is used in high level languages. Using the Assembler, the executable code is generated (in a file) which is used for producing the corresponding results. In the case of MIPS Assembly, the "interpretation" procedure for producing the final executable code is implemented exclusively within the simulation environment. Figure 1.3 shows the above procedure.

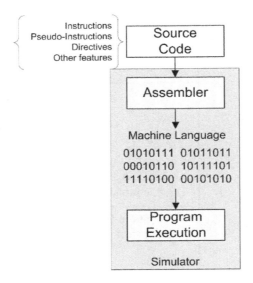

Figure 1.3 From source code to machine language

On the other hand, for developing operational Assembly programs for the MIPS microprocessor, some programming components are also required:

(a) Instructions or/and pseudo-instructions of the symbolic language (Assembly)

The MIPS programming is achieved by using the available instructions ("normal" instructions or pseudo-instructions). The "normal" instructions are "translated" directly to machine language and the pseudo-instructions are "translated" to "normal" instructions for producing the final executable code. At code development level, the available instruction set contains "normal" as well as "pseudo" instructions. For simplicity reasons, the general term "instructions" will be used for all the instruction types.

(b) Directives (or special commands) to the MIPS microprocessor (within the simulation environment)
These directives do not constitute instructions and are used for giving additional information for the program regarding the code and data areas, the text massages, etc.

(c) Functions for specific program operations
Functions constitute complete subprograms that extend the main program functionality by offering useful operations such as keyboard reading, message displaying, etc.

In the next sections, the most important instructions will be presented as well as the corresponding examples.

1.4.1 Load and Store instructions
In this category there are instructions for loading/storing (from/to) arithmetic values or register contents to registers or memory locations, etc. Moreover, the data size for memory operations can be defined by the programmer. It is known that the conventional memory model hosts 8bits (1 byte) of data in each memory location. As mentioned in previous section, each register has a capacity of 32bits (4 bytes). This means that the content of four memory locations can be stored in a register. Thus, the data size for transfer operations (from/to memory) has to be defined. Through the above operations, the memory addressing methods will be also presented.

Loading an integer value to a register
The data loading to a register may has different sources such as registers, an integer value or memory locations. Despite the fact that the assignment operation is always the same, a different Assembly instruction is needed in each case. As an example it is assumed that in C language, the programmer has developed the following assignments:

A=5;
B=C;

The above assignments are usual and are described by the programmer with the same way. More precisely, there is an assignment of a numeric value and an assignment of another variable. This difference is not a problem for the C language. On the other hand, in MIPS Assembly, the above assignments require different instructions.

For loading an integer value to a register, the instruction li (load immediate) will be used as follows:

```
li Rdest,imm
```

where Rdest is the destination register (where the value will be stored) and imm the integer value (signed/unsigned integers 16 or 32 bits).

Example

Before

Register	Content
$v0	?

```
li $v0,4
```

After

Register	Content
$v0	04

Finally $v0=4.

The symbol "?" represents an existing (previous) but unknown value. In other words, before the execution of the instruction li $v0,4, the register $v0 had some content that is replaced by the new value.

When a loading of an integer value takes place, the corresponding limitations have to be known because affect the data integrity. For the previous case, a possible question is what does the 16 bits signed value mean in terms of maximum values, etc. In the case of 16 bits signed values, the first bit is used as a sign bit and the rest of the bits (15 bits) represent the magnitude. Due to the fact that the system uses the two's complement for representing signed numbers, the corresponding range is [-32768,32767]. For unsigned numbers the above range becomes [0,65535].

Loading a register from another register

The loading type (data source), determines the corresponding instruction. Thus, if both source and destination are registers, the instruction move is used.

```
move Rdest, Rsrc
```

Rdest is the register (destination) where the content of Rsrc will be stored (through copy).

Example

Before

Register	Content
$t1	0A

Register	Content
$t2	?

```
move $t2,$t1
```

After

Register	Content
$t1	0A

Register	Content
$t2	0A

In other words, the assignment $t2=$t1 will be performed.

Loading an address to a register

For supporting efficiently the program development, labels are used for defining specific points within the code. These labels can be used for driving the execution flow in a specific instruction in the case of an iteration (loop), etc. Each label corresponds to a real memory address. This address has to be known in some cases (e.g. displaying a text message from the data area). For loading the real address of a label in a register, the instruction la (load address) is used. With the instruction

```
la Rdest,varLabel
```

the corresponding address of the label `varLabel` is stored in `Rdest`.

Example

```
la $a0,mymessage
```

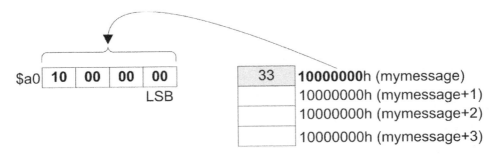

Figure 1.4 Loading the real address of a label

The above operation can be written with a symbolic way as `$a0=mymessage`

Loading data from the main memory
Due to the fact that every register is 4 bytes (32 bits) wide, the content of four successive memory locations can be stored. The number of bytes (1-4) to read from memory and store in the register can be defined by the corresponding Assembly instruction. For example, only two bytes of the register can be loaded from the memory.
Obviously, if the corresponding number is signed or not, it must be known for using the correct arithmetic representation.

For loading only one byte from a single memory location, the following instruction will be used:

```
lb Rdest, address
```

`Rdest` is the destination register where the content of the memory location `address` will be stored. The above address can be expressed with the corresponding hexadecimal number.

Example

Before

Register	Content
$t1	?

```
lb $t1, arrayA
```

After

Register	Content
$t1	33

Figure 1.5 shows the operation of the above instruction. The content of the memory location which corresponds to the label arrayA, is copied to the least significant byte of the register $t1 (the label corresponds to a real memory address). In this example, the number 33 (content of the memory location arrayA) is copied to the register.

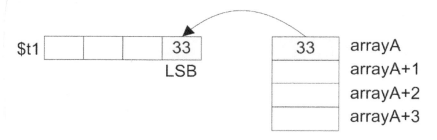

Figure 1.5 Loading a byte from a symbolic address

In the next example, the loading of the register is performed directly by defining a real memory address (the prefix 0x is used for denoting a hexadecimal number). In this example it is assumed that the label arrayA corresponds to the real address 0x10000000.

Before

Register	Content
$t1	?

```
lb $t1,0x10000000
```

After

Register	Content
$t1	33

With the above instruction the operation $t1=[0x10000000] is performed

Figure 1.6 shows the operation of the instruction where a real memory address is used.

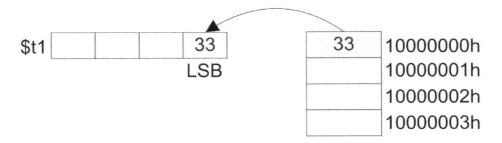

Figure 1.6 Loading a byte by using a real memory address

Load instructions have three variations:

(a) lb Rdest,address (loading Rdest from a memory location (1 byte) with address address)

(b) lh Rdest,address (loading Rdest from two successive memory locations (2 bytes), starting from the address address)

(c) lw Rdest,address (loading Rdest from four successive memory locations (4 bytes), starting from the address address)

(b=byte=8bits, h=half word=16bits, w=word=32bits).

There are various methods to express the address address. These methods are based on the addressing modes of the microprocessor.

Storing data in the main memory
The opposite of the loading operation is the storing operation. Like in loading, the corresponding data size (byte, halfword, word) for storing can be also specified. In other words, the number of bytes from a register that will be stored in successive memory locations can be specified by the Assembly instruction.
For storing one byte from a register to a memory location, the instruction sb (store byte) will be used in the following form:

```
sb Rsrc, address
```

Figure 1.7 shows the difference between loading and storing operations. With loading operation, the content of a register is loaded from one or more successive memory locations and with storing operation the content of a register is stored in one or more successive memory locations.

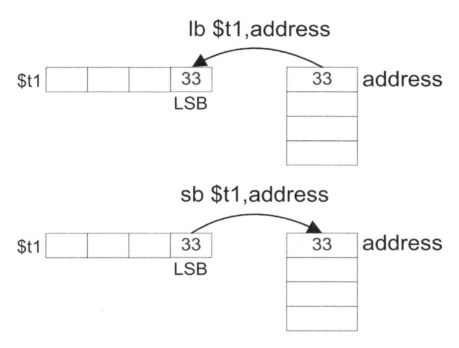

Figure 1.7 Difference between loading and storing operation for 1 byte data

The variations of storing operations are as follows:

(a) sb Rdest,address (storing the least significant byte of Rdest (1 byte) in the memory location address)

(b) sh Rdest,address (storing the two least significant bytes of Rdest in two successive memory locations starting from the address address)

(c) sw Rdest,address (storing the content of Rdest in four successive memory locations starting from the address address)
(b=byte=8bits, h=half word=16bits, w=word=32bits).

Figure 1.8 shows the loading and storing operations for 4 bytes of data (whole register).

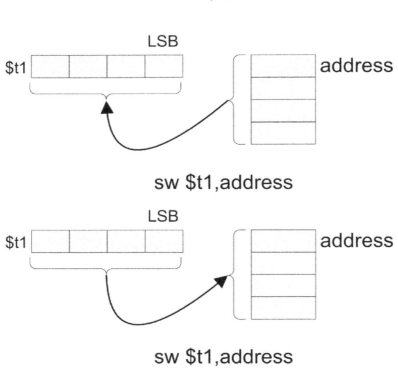

Figure 1.8 shows also that the register content (4 bytes) corresponds to four successive memory locations.

Table 1.1 summarizes the load and store instructions.

Table 1.1 Load and Store instructions	
li *Rdest,imm*	Loading in **Rdest** the integer value ***imm***
la *Rdest,mymessage*	Loading in **Rdest** the corresponding address of the label ***mymessage***
move *Rdest,Rsrc*	Loading in **Rdest** the content of **Rsrc** *(through copy)*
lb *Rdest,address*	Loading in **Rdest** one byte (8 bits) which is stored in the address ***address***. It is assumed that the number is signed (sign information in the rest three bytes of **Rdest**)
lbu *Rdest,address*	Unsigned loading in **Rdest** (LSB) of the byte (8 bits) which is stored in the address ***address***
lh *Rdest,address*	Loading in **Rdest** of the half word (16 bits), starting from the address ***address***. It is assumed that the number is signed (sign information in the rest of the bytes of **Rdest**)
lhu *Rdest,address*	Unsigned loading in **Rdest** of a half word (16 bits), starting from the address ***address***
lw *Rdest,address*	Loading in **Rdest** of a word (32 bits), starting from the address ***address***
sb *Rsrc,address*	Storing of the least significant byte (8 bits) of **Rsrc** in the memory location ***address***
sh *Rsrc,address*	Storing the least significant half word (16 bits) from **Rsrc** in memory starting from the address ***address***
sw *Rsrc,address*	Storing a word (32 bits) from **Rsrc** in memory starting from the address ***address***

The need for more addressing methods

Assume that a data collection exists in successive memory locations (`address`, `address+1`, `address+2`, etc). It must be exists a way for managing the data flexibly. This means that a loop has to be developed together with the starting address and a deviation pointer for accessing the data. The above need drives to the supported addressing methods of the microprocessor. These methods will be practically analyzed in next chapters.

1.4.2 Arithmetic instructions

Arithmetic instructions support the four basic math operations under specific rules and limitations. In the basic form of math operations, three arguments are used. The corresponding operation is performed between the second and the third argument, while the result is stored in the first argument. The four math operations that are based on specific Assembly instructions, are:

(a) `add Rdest, Rsrc1, Rsrc2` (summation calculation `Rsrc1+Rsrc2` result in `Rdest`, i.e. `Rdest= Rsrc1+Rsrc2`)

(b) `sub Rdest, Rsrc1, Rsrc2` (subtraction calculation `Rsrc1-Rsrc2` result in `Rdest`, i.e. `Rdest= Rsrc1-Rsrc2`)

(c) `mul Rdest, Rsrc1, Rsrc2` (product calculation `Rsrc1*Rsrc2` result in `Rdest`, i.e. `Rdest= Rsrc1*Rsrc2`)

(d) `div Rdest, Rsrc1, Rsrc2` (division calculation (quotient) `Rsrc1/Rsrc2` result in `Rdest`, i.e. `Rdest= Rsrc1/Rsrc2`)

The argument `Rsrc2` can be an integer number

Finally, the math operation rules, are:

1. Calculation between second and third argument

2. Result storage in the first argument

3. Firstly, the calculation is performed (step 1) and secondly the result is stored in the first argument

4. When the desired operation has more than two numbers, then the calculation is performed by using more than one Assembly instructions

Addition (summation)

Example 1

Calculating the $t1+$t2

Before

Register	Content
$t1	1

Register	Content
$t2	5

```
add $t0,$t1,$t2
```

After

Register	Content
$t1	1

Register	Content
$t2	5

Register	Content
$t0	6

The same addition can be performed by using $t1 for storing the result

```
add $t1,$t1,$t2
```

After

Register	Content
$t2	5

Register	Content
$t1	6

Example 2

Assume that the addition $t1+$t2+$t3 ($t1=2, $t2=3, $t3=4) will be calculated. All the math operations can be performed only between two numbers. Thus, multiple addition instructions have to be used as follows:

```
add $t0,$t1,$t2       #$t0=$t1+$t2
add $t0,$t0,$t3       #$t0=$t0+$t3=($t1+$t2)+$t3=$t1+$t2+$t3
```

Note: any text that follows the character '#', is a comment

Initially, the addition between $t1 and $t2 is performed and the result is stored in $t0. Next, $t0 (contains already $t1+$t2) is added with $t3 and thus, the required calculation is completed ($t1+$t2+$t3).

The above operation step by step is as follows:

Step 1
$t1 and $t2 are added with the instruction add $t0,$t1,$t2. Thus, $t0 will be

Register	Content
$t0	5

Step 2
$t0 (contains already $t1+$t2) is added with $t3. The final content of $t0 will be

Register	Content
$t0	9

If $t1 is used for storing the results, the above instructions are formed as follows:

```
add $t1,$t1,$t2
add $t1,$t1,$t3
```

initially the summation is stored in $t1, and then, $t3 is added.

Subtraction

In subtraction the arguments order is critical due to the fact that the third argument is subtracted from the second one. Different results are produced from the calculations $t1-$t2 and $t2-$t1.

Example 1

Assuming $t1=5 and $t2=3, the calculations $t1-$t2 and $t2-$t1 will be performed.

```
sub $t0,$t1,$t2
```

after the execution of the above instruction, the content of $t0 will be

Register	Content
$t0	2

due to the fact that the operation 5-3 is performed.

The instruction `sub $t0,$t2,$t1`

Will give as a result:

Register	Content
$t0	-2

due to the fact that the operation 3-5 is performed. The representation of number -2 is based on the two's complement.

Example 2

The implementation of the operation $t1-$t2-$t3 will be developed by executing the following instructions:

```
sub $t0,$t1,$t2
sub $t0,$t0,$t3
```

Multiplication (product)
For calculating $t1*$t2, the following instruction will be used

```
mul $t0,$t1,$t2
```

if $t1=3 and $t2=5, then $t0=15

For calculating the product 3*$t1, the following instruction is needed:

`mul $t0,$t1,3` (the integer value can be placed only as the third argument within the instruction)

Division

The instruction `div $t0,$t1,$t2` performs the division $t1/$t2 and the quotient (result) is stored in the first argument ($t0) like in other math operations. Please note that only the integer part of the result is stored.

Other forms of math operations

There is one more variation of the `div` instruction. In this new variation, the quotient and the remainder is calculated based on the integer division. The `div` instruction in this case is expressed by using only two arguments:

`div Rsrc1,Rsrc2`

the microprocessor calculates `Rsrc1/Rsrc2` and the remainder and quotient are stored in the special purpose registers `HI` and `LO` respectively. As mentioned before, the registers `HI` and `LO` hosts only the result of multiplication or division instructions. This means that the registers `HI` and `LO` cannot be used directly as the general purpose registers. Thus, there are special instructions for extracting the content of these registers in a general purpose register for further processing. The next instruction copies the content of the register `HI` in the desired general purpose register.

`mfhi Rdest` (`mfhi` means: move from `HI`)

the above operation can be written as `Rdest=[HI]`

for extracting the content of `LO`, the following instruction is used:

`mflo Rdest` (`mflo` means: move from `LO`)

the above operation can be written as `Rdest=[LO]`

Example
If $t1=5 and $t2=2, then the instruction `div $t1,$t2` will give

Register	Content
HI	1

Register	Content
LO	2

`mflo $t3`

Register	Content
$t3	2

Another special math instruction is `neg` which inverts the sign of a number inside a register. In other words, the content of the register is multiplied with -1 and the result is stored in a second register.

The above instruction is expressed as follows:

`neg Rdest,Rsrc` (multiplication of `Rsrc` with -1 and result storage in `Rdest`)

Example
If $t1=1, then the instruction

`neg $t0,$t1`

will give

Register	Content
$t0	-1

Table 1.2 contains the available math instructions that are supported by the MIPS Assembly.

Table 1.2 Math instructions

`add Rdest, Rsrc1, Src`	Rdest = Rsrc1 + Src
`addi Rdest, Rsrc1, Imm`	Rdest = Rsrc1 + Imm
`sub Rdest, Rsrc1, Src2`	Rdest = Rsrc1 - Src2
`mul Rdest, Rsrc1, Src2`	Rdest = Rsrc1 * Src2
`div Rdest, Rsrc1, Src2`	Rdest = Rsrc1 / Src2 (quotient)
`div Rsrc1, Rsrc2`	Rsrc1 / Rsrc2, HI=remainder, LO=quotient
`rem Rdest, Rsrc1, Rsrc2`	Rdest = Rsrc1 / Src2 (remainder)
`mult Rsrc1, Rsrc2`	Rsrc1* Rsrc2 , LO=low order word, HI=high order word
`neg Rdest, Rsrc`	Rdest = - Rsrc. Sign inversion of Rsrc and result storage in Rdest
`abs Rdest,Rsrc`	Absolute value calculation of Rsrc and result storage in Rdest

`Src2` can be a register or a numerical value

1.4.3 Control flow and branch-jump instructions (conditionals)

In most of the programs there is a need for instructions execution under specific conditions. In MIPS Assembly, every condition check is expressed together with a label, where the execution flow will be driven if the condition is true. As compared to a high level language, a TRUE case in Assembly drives the execution flow to another code section where the corresponding label is defined. A classic implementation of a condition-decision case in C language, will has the following form:

```
if (condition)
     {instructions for the TRUE case}
else
     { instructions for the FALSE case }
```

In Assembly language the corresponding implementation has the following logic:

```
if (condition-true) goto section LABEL
Instructions of the FALSE case
```

In the above implementation, if the condition is TRUE, then the execution flow is driven to section which starts from the point LABEL, otherwise (FALSE case) the following instructions (after the condition check) are executed.

The condition may involve a comparison with zero, any other number or the content of a register. These instructions start with the letter 'b' which is followed from two letters that denote the type of comparison and are completed with two or three arguments. If the comparison will be performed with zero, the following two arguments are used:

(a) register name (for comparing its content)
(b) label for branch-jump if the condition is TRUE

In the case of a register comparison with a register, the following three arguments are used:

(a) the name of the first register
(b) the name of the second register (or a number)
(c) label for branch-jump if the condition is TRUE

Tables 1.3 and 1.4 show the two condition-check instruction groups that already mentioned.

Table 1.3 Instructions for flow control and branch-jump
(comparison with zero)

beqz Rsrc, label	Branch-jump to label if Rsrc = 0
bgez Rsrc, label	Branch-jump to label if Rsrc>= 0
bgtz Rsrc, label	Branch-jump to label if Rsrc> 0
blez Rsrc, label	Branch-jump to label if Rsrc<= 0
bltz Rsrc, label	Branch-jump to label if Rsrc< 0
bnez Rsrc, label	Branch-jump to label if Rsrc<> 0

Table 1.4
Instructions for flow control and branch-jump
(comparison with register or number)

beq Rsrc, Src, label	Branch-jump to label if Rsrc = Src
bge Rsrc, Src, label	Branch-jump to label if Rsrc>= Src
bgt Rsrc, Src, label	Branch-jump to label if Rsrc>Src
ble Rsrc, Src, label	Branch-jump to label if Rsrc<= Src
blt Rsrc, Src, label	Branch-jump to label if Rsrc<Src
bne Rsrc, Src, label	Branch-jump to label if Rsrc<>Src

Src can be a register or an integer value. Branch instructions use signed 16-bits deviation (2^{15}-1 *instructions (not bytes) forward or* 2^{15} instructions backwards).

The symbols that follow the letter 'b' are based on the condition-check type (table 1.5).

Table 1.5
Symbols for condition-check

eq	equal (=)
ge	greater equal (>=)
gt	greater than (>)
le	less equal (<=)
lt	less than (<)
ne	not equal (≠)

Branch-jump instructions without condition-check (unconditional)
In some cases, the execution flow has to be driven to a specific code section without any conditional check. Such a case is when a code section has to be avoided. Table 1.6 shows these instructions.

Table 1.6 Branch-jump instructions without condition-check

b label	Branch to label
j label	Jump to label
jal label	Jump to label (storage of the return address in $31 or $ra)
jr Rsrc	Jump to instruction that corresponds to the address which is defined by the content of Rsrc (without condition-check) (jr $31 or jr $ra for returning from a subprogram which has called with the instruction jal label)

Instruction j (jump) has a 26 bits address field

Example 1
Assume that a program checks the content of $t1. If $t1=10, then the value 4 will be assigned to $t2, otherwise the value 3.

```
beq
$t1,10,timi4
li $t2,3
j L2
timi4:
li $t2,4
L2:
```

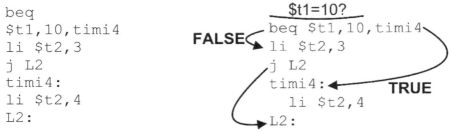

Figure 1.9 Checking a register content and branching

As shown in figure 1.9, a comparison of $t1 with 10 is performed. If the content of $t1 is equal to 10 (TRUE case), then a branch to label timi4 is performed and the execution flow is continued from that point (the number 4 is assigned to $t2). Otherwise, (FALSE case), no branch is performed to label timi4 and the execution flow is continued from the next instruction which assigns the number 3 to $t2. The instruction j L2 drives directly the control flow to label L2 in order to avoid the code section which starts from the label timi4 and belongs to the TRUE case. Figure 1.10 shows the flow chart for the above code.

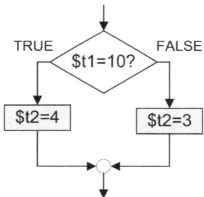

Figure 1.10 Flow chart diagram (controlling the execution flow)

Example 2

A program checks if $t1=0 and $t2>=5. If this is TRUE, then the assignment $t0=1 is performed, otherwise nothing (execution flow continues from the label L2). Due to the fact that MIPS Assembly does not support complex conditions-checks, two different checks have to be developed. The whole condition-check is TRUE only if both the conditions-checks are also TRUE. Thus, if the first condition-check is TRUE, then a second check has to be performed for the expression $t2>=5. If any of the two conditions-checks is FALSE, then the whole condition-check expression is FALSE.

```
li $t0,0          #$t0=0
beq $t1,0,syn1    #If $t1=0, then goto syn1
j L2              #Goto L2 (unconditional)

syn1:             #Point syn1
bge $t2,5,syn2    #If $t2>=5, then goto syn2
j L2              #Goto L2 (unconditional), for
                  #avoiding section syn2

syn2:             #Point syn2
li $t0,1          #$t0=1
L2:               #Point L2
```

Figure 1.11 shows all the possible execution flows based on the corresponding conditions-checks. The register $t0 has the initial value 0. If both conditions-checks are TRUE, then the new content of $t0 is 1. In other words, if both conditions-checks are TRUE, then the execution flow is driven to the point syn2. If $t1=0 then the execution flow is driven to syn1 and if $t2>=5, then the execution is driven to syn2 where the value 1 is assigned to $t0.

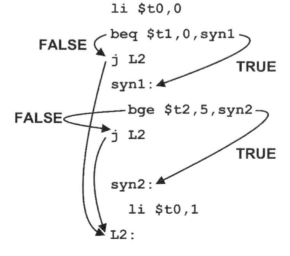

Figure 1.11 Execution flows

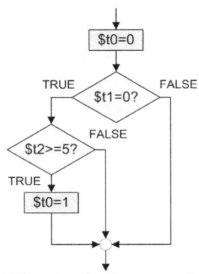

Figure 1.12 Flow chart for the two conditions-checks

Figure 1.12 shows that if at least one condition-check is FALSE, then the instruction which assigns the number 1 to $t0 is avoided.

1.4.4 Implementing multiple conditions-checks and iteration loops

In this section, some basic conditions-checks regarding more decisions will be presented. For simplicity reasons, the corresponding C implementation will be initially analyzed.

Simple control flow (condition-check) `if-then-else`

In simple condition-check, only one case is examined. Based on the condition-check result, two mutual excluded code sections will be activated (TRUE and FALSE cases). Assume that the content of a variable is compared to zero. The implementation in C language can be performed with the following approaches (code (a) and (b)):

```
if (i==0)                      if (i!=0)
  {//TRUE case ins.              {//FALSE case ins.
   //i=0}                        //but for TRUE condition
else                            //i≠0}
  {//FALSE case ins.          else
   //i≠0}                       {//TRUE case ins.
                                //but for FALSE condition
                                //i=0}


        Code (a)                       Code (b)
```

In Assembly language the content of a register is checked. Like the above implementations, the conditions-checks in Assembly will be similarly developed (Code (c) and (d)):

```
#Check $t0
beqz $t0, L1
#FALSE case
#$t0 is not equal to 0
j L2


L1:
#TRUE case
#$t0 is equal to 0
L2:
```

```
#Check $t0
bnez $t0, L1
#FALSE case
#$t0 is equal to 0
j L2


L1:
#TRUE case
#$t0 is not equal to 0
L2:
```

Code (c)   **Code (d)**

In code (c) the content of $t0 is initially checked. if $t0 is equal to 0 (TRUE case), then the execution flow is driven to L1, otherwise the execution flow is continued from the instruction bellow the condition-check (FALSE case). In second implementation (code (d)), the opposite condition-checked is performed. If $t0 is not equal to 0 (TRUE case) then the execution flow is driven to L1, otherwise the next instruction is executed (below the condition-check). Note that in both cases, there is an unconditional jump to L2 for avoiding the instructions of the second case. This may be happened due to the fact that the labels do not change the execution flow. Figures 1.13a and 1.13b show the flow chart for the two implementation approaches.

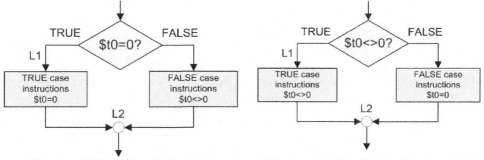

Figure 1.13a Check if equal   **Figure 1.13b** Check if not equal

Double condition-check `if-then-if`

In double condition-check, there are two conditions that are logically "connected" through an AND or an OR. For presenting the double condition-check, it is assumed that a program will check if the content of a register belongs in the range [10,20]. A number belongs to a closed range (the upper and lower number are included) only if two conditions-checks are TRUE at the same time (one condition-check for the lower limit and one condition-check for the upper limit). The above conditions are logically "connected" with an AND. Obviously, the whole condition-check can be performed with the opposite logic. In other words, the condition-check can be performed by checking if the content of the register does not belong to the given range. In such a case, if the content is less than the lower limit or is greater than the upper limit, then the content does not belong to that range. In C language the above condition-check can be implemented with a single IF where the two conditions are included. On the other hand, in Assembly language implementation two separate conditions-checks have to be developed. For the above reasons, two separate conditions-checks will be initially implemented also in C language.

```
if (i>=10)                    if (i<10)
    if ((i<=20))                  {//does not belong}
        {//belongs}           else
    else                          if (i>20)
    {//does not belong}              {//does not belong}
else                          else
{does not belong}                {//belongs}
```

First approach (check if belongs)   **Second approach**
(check if not belongs)

Based on the first approach, the left (lower) limit will be initially checked. If this condition-check is TRUE ($i>=10$), then the first requirement is fulfilled and the checking process will be continued for the right (upper) limit (check if $i<=20$). If any of the above conditions-checks is FALSE, then the number is definitely out of the given range. In the second approach, the initial step is to check if the number is out of the range from the left side (lower limit). If $i<10$, then the number does not belong to that range. If $i<10$ is not TRUE, then the truth is that $i>=10$ and thus the second check has to be performed. If $i>20$ is not TRUE, then the truth is that $i<=20$. For reaching that check, means that previously i>=10. Thus, if i>=10 and i<=20, then the number belongs to the given range.

The following code shows the corresponding implementation in Assembly language.

```
bge $t0,10,aok          blt $t0,10,L1
j L1                    bgt $t0,20,L1
aok:                    #belongs
ble $t0,20,bok          j L2
j L1                    L1:
bok:                    #does not belong
#belongs                L2:
  j L2
L1:
  #does not belong
L2:
```

| **First approach** | **Second approach** |
| (check if belongs) | (check if not belongs) |

Triple condition-check

In this type there are three possibilities that can be checked by using two or three conditions-checks. Assume that a number is examined if is positive, negative or zero. In this case, three possibilities exist. Looking for the optimal code, only two checks have to be implemented for the above case, because if two of the checks are FALSE, then the third check is TRUE. For studying better the optimal coding, two different implementations (approaches) have been made.

```
if (i>0)                if (i>0)
  {//positive}            {//positive}
else                    else
if (i<0)                if (i<0)
    {//negative}            {//negative}
  else                    else
    if (i==0)               {//zero}
      {//zero}
```

| **Three checks** (redundancy) | **Two checks** (optimal code) |

Both approaches will be implemented in Assembly language. It is assumed that for every case a corresponding message will be displayed (comment in the following code).

```
beqz $t1,zer
bgtz $t1,pos
#else
#Display "negative"
j L1

zer:
#Display "zero"
j L1

pos:
#Display "positive"

L1:
#Exit
```

Initially, the number (content of $t1) is compared to zero. If this is TRUE, then the execution flow is driven to zer and the other messages are avoided. If the number is positive, then the first condition-check is FALSE and the execution flow is continued from the bgtz. If this condition-check is TRUE, then the corresponding message will be displayed and the execution flow will be continued from L1.

Finally, if no one of the conditions-checks is TRUE then the execution flow does not reach the points zer or pos and the message "negative" will be displayed.

Figure 1.14 shows the possible execution flows. Always remember that the FALSE case is represented by the instruction which is after the condition-check. With j L1 the unwanted code sections are avoided. For example, when the number is negative, the corresponding message is displayed and the execution flow is driven to exit (L1). Without the above instruction, the program will display also the message "zero" that belongs to a different case. Due to the fact that always only one condition-check is TRUE, the messages display is mutual excluded.

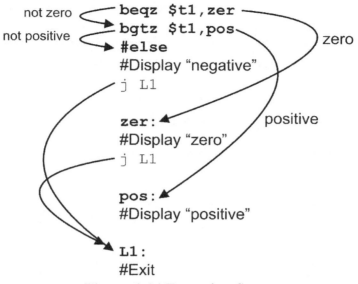

Figure 1.14 Execution flows

Iteration loop `do-while`

For developing iteration loops a condition-check has to be included in order to control (continue or stop) the iterations. In current implementation (do-while) the inner instructions are executed at least one time before the condition check. The do-while loop is the most popular in Assembly language due to the fact that can be developed easily and corresponds directly to the C language instructions logic. In the next code the C implementation is presented as well as the MIPS Assembly.

```
x=1;                    li $t0,1

do                      start:

{

//Instructions         #Instructions
//that will be         #that will be
//repeated             #repeated

x++;                    add $t0,$t0,1

}
while (x<=15);          ble $t0,15,start


do-while in C          do-while in Assembly
```

Based on the above code form, the algorithm philosophy never changes. The loop basic components such as the counter, the counter update and the condition-check are always needed independently of the language implementation (C or Assembly).

Iteration loop `while-do`

In this case, the corresponding Assembly implementation requires more instructions for controlling the execution flow due to the fact that the loop control has to be placed at the beginning before the inner instructions. The following code is indicative.

```
x=1;                              li $t0,1

while (x<=15)                     start:
{                                 ble $t0,15,next
                                  j cont
//Instructions
//that will be                    next:
//repeated
                                  #Instructions
x++;                              #that will be repeated


}                                 add $t0,$t0,1
                                  j start

                                  cont:
                                  #Program continue
```

while-do in C   **while-do in Assembly**

In the Assembly program, the counter initialization is firstly performed and then, the condition-check is implemented in order to control the loop. If the condition-check `ble $t0,15,next` is TRUE, then the execution flow is driven inside the loop for executing the inner instructions. If the condition-check is FALSE, the branch-jump to the point `next` is avoided and the execution flow is continued from the next instruction (`j cont`). After the counter update the execution flow is returned to the initial condition-check (`j start`).

The flow charts of figure 1.15 show the differences of the above iteration loop types at algorithm level.

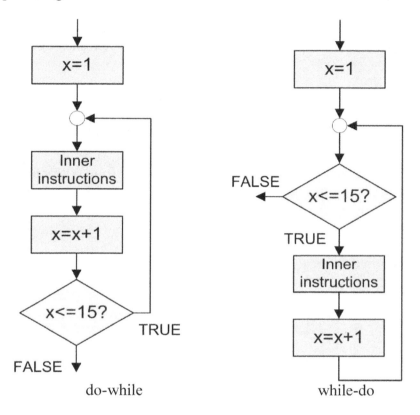

do-while   while-do

Figure 1.15 Flow charts for the iteration loops

1.4.5 Developing the first operational program

Until now, only the required code sections for implementing basic programming structures have been analyzed. In this section, the methods for developing fully operational Assembly programs (inside simulator) will be presented. For achieving that, additional directives and functions will be used.

Directives

Directives constitute specific instructions (not Assembly) to the execution system environment (simulation environment). For the above reason, they start with the special character '.'. The basic directives are:

```
.text
```

Defines the starting point of the code area and is expressed together with a starting memory address.

`.data`
Defines the starting point of the data area (e.g. hosting the text messages).

`.ascii string`
Declares the alphanumeric `string` (e.g. `msg_label:` `.ascii` "hello"), where `msg_label` is a label for referring to the string.

`.asciiz string`
Declares the alphanumeric `string` which is followed from a termination character (e.g. `msg_label:` `.asciiz` "hello"), where `msg_label` is a label for referring to the string.

`.space n`
Reserves n bytes in data area

`.align n`
Data organization in groups of 2^n. This directive is used in the arrays management.

Finally, there are directives such as `.half`, `.word`, etc for declaring numerical data

Functions
Functions make the programs fully operational due to the fact that offer more capabilities such as keyboard read, message display, etc. All the available functions are called with a typical way and the necessary arguments have to be used. These arguments are passed to functions through specific registers. On the other hand, the produced results are also available through registers. Thus, for using the basic functions, the following table is used (table 1.7):

Table 1.7 Available functions

Function	Unique function number (ID) Always in $v0	Input (arguments)	Output (results)	Calling method
print string (screen)	4	$a0 = message address	Display string on screen	```li $v0,4 la a0,mymessage syscall```
print integer (screen)	1	$a0 = number to be displayed	Display an integer number on screen	```li $v0,1 move $a0,Rsrc syscall # load $a0 from a register (Rsrc) or``` ```li $v0,1 li $a0,Imm syscall #load $a0 with an integer value (Imm)```
read integer (keyboard)	5	-	$v0 = the number from the kayboard	```li $v0,5 syscall```
read string (keyboard)	8	$a0 = starting address for storing the string (e.g. myspace) $a1=number of characters to be read	-	```li $v0,8 la $a0,myspace li $a1,n```
Exit (program termination)	10	-	-	```li $v0,10 syscall```

The instruction `syscall` is used for activating the function call after the arguments preparation (e.g. function number in $v0 and other needed arguments in the corresponding registers).

Program framework

For developing any program some minimum components are needed. These components are the code section and the exit function (program termination). Thus, the minimum components for any program are formed as follows:

```
#Code section
.text 0x00400000

#Main Instructions
#are placed here

#Exit
li $v0,10
syscall
```

HelloWorld!!

The first program displays on screen the message HelloWorld!!. After the message the program is terminated. Moreover the message has to be declared in the data area. Thus, the program structure logic is as follows:

Code section
Display message (function 4)
Termination (function 10)

Data section
Message declaration

The following code constitutes the implementation of the above logic.

```
#Code section
.text 0x00400000

#Display message (function 4)
li $v0,4
la $a0,mymessage
syscall

#Termination (function 10)
li $v0,10
syscall
```

```
#Data section
.data

#Message declaration
mymessage: .asciiz "Hello World!!"
```

Figure 1.16 shows the stored message in memory as well as the operation of the instruction li $a0,mymessage.

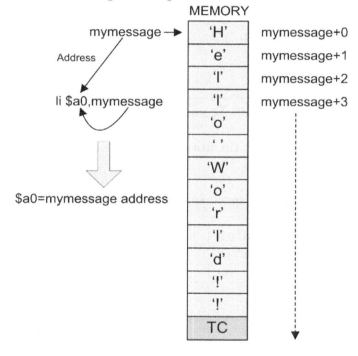

Figure 1.16 The message in memory

In memory locations of figure 1.16, the ASCII code of every message character is stored. For simplicity reasons, only the corresponding ASCII characters (in quotation marks) are presented in the above figure. The label mymessage corresponds to a real constant memory address. This address corresponds only to one memory location and not in all the message locations. The function 4 (print string) starts to scan the message from the address mymessage until the termination character (TC). This character has been automatically placed at the end of the string because the directive .asciiz is used (the .ascii does not place a termination character). Through the instruction `li $a0,mymessage`, the address of the label `mymessage` is loaded in `$a0`. This means that the system 'converts' the label to a real memory address.

With the above example the form of an array within the memory is also presented. The message represents a 14 bytes array starting from the address `mymessage`. For accessing the array elements, the starting address is required in combination with a pointer for calculating the distance (deviation in bytes) from the above address. Thus, the first array location will has the address `mymessage+0` (deviation 0 from the location `mymessage`), the second will has the address `mymessage+1`, etc. Due to the fact that any array is implemented in the main memory, all the arrays will have the same form of figure 1.16 (an one dimension array).

Exercises for chapter 1

1.1 The registers of the MIPS 32 microprocessor are _____ bits

1.2 For non signed integers, the maximum value that can be hosted by a register is _____

1.3 The message 'Hello' is stored in memory in the following form:

Symbol	Address	Content
msg	540A	'H'
		'e'
		'l'
		'l'
		'o'

(a) fill the rest addresses that correspond to message characters

(b) write the content of $a0 if the instruction la $a0,msg is executed

1.4 Assume that a logic array hosts the content of four registers. If the registers storage starts from the address 5FF0, write the starting address for every register.

1.5 Develop a code section for loading the number 12 in $t0 and calculating $t0+$t1+2*($t0)

1.6 Write an instruction for loading the result of exercise 1.5 in $t4

1.7 Develop code for the following calculations:
(a) (2*$t1)/$t2
(b) ($t1-$t2) mod $t0
(c) $t2^2-4*$t1*$t3
(d) ($t1-$t2)*(3*$t4)

1.8 Develop code for calculating (3*$t1)-$t4 if $t0>0 and $t2/$t1 if $t0<0

1.9 Write a complete program for reading an integer number from the keyboard and displaying that number on the screen.

1.10 Develop a code section for calculating A+B-2AB, where A and B are implemented by registers of your choice.

1.11 Develop code for the following calculation:
(2*$t1)/(2*$t2^3)

1.12 Develop code for calculating (3*$t1)-$t4 if ($t0>0 and $t2>10)

1.13 Implement in MIPS Assembly the following code of C language

```
{
        if (i==j) f = f + g;
        else f = f * 2;
}
```

1.14 Implement in MIPS Assembly the following code of C language

```
{
        if (i==j)
                if (i>10) i = i + 1;
        elsei = i-1;
}
```

1.15 Write the corresponding C code of the following instructions

```
add $t0, $t1, $t2
sub $t0,$t0,2
mul $t1,$t1,$t2
add $t0,$t0,$t0
```

1.16 Write the corresponding C code for the instruction add $s0, $s1, $s2

1.17 Implement in MIPS Assembly the following code of C language

```
{
printf("hello\n");
}
```

1.18 Implement in MIPS Assembly the following code of C language

```
{
int i=5;
printf("%d",i);
}
```

1.19 Write the corresponding C code for the following Assembly code

```
li $v0,5        #function select
syscall         #function call
move $t1,$v0
```

1.20 Implement in MIPS Assembly the following code of C language

```
{
if (i==0)
        printf("hello\n");
}
```

1.21 Implement in MIPS Assembly the following code of C language

```
{
i=5; j=4
i=i+j
if (i<>j)
        printf("%d",i);
}
```

1.22 Write the corresponding C code for the following Assembly code

```
li $v0,5        #function select
syscall         #function call
move $t1,$v0
add $t1,$t1,$t1
```

1.23 Write the result on screen for the following program

```
li $t0,1
again:
        move $a0,$t0
        add $a0,$a0,$t0
        li $v0,1
        syscall
        add $t0,$t0,1
        move $t2,$t0
ble $t2,10,again
```

1.24 Find the error in the following program and write the corresponding corrections.

```
li $t0,10
again:
        li $t0,1
        move $a0,$t0
        add $a0,$a0,$t0
        li $v0,1
        syscall
        add $t0,$t0,1
        move $t2,$t0
ble $t2,10,again
```

1.25 Write the result on the screen when the following program is executed

```
li $t0,10
li $t1,4
again:
        div$t0,$t1
        move $a0,$t0
        add $a0,$a0,$t0
```

```
        li $v0,1
        syscall
        add $t0,$t0,1
        move $t2,$t0
ble $t2,10,again
```

1.26 In the following C program, an integer is read from the keyboard and is displayed on screen. Moreover, before the number read, a help message is displayed. Write the corresponding program in MIPS Assembly.

```
int main ()
{
int i;
printf("dose i:");
scanf("%d",&i);
printf("\ni=%d",i);
return 0;
}
```

The main points of the chapter

MIPS 32bit registers
The MIPS microprocessor has 32 general purpose registers, two special purpose for arithmetic operations and a program counter. Every register corresponds to a unique number (identifier) and inside programs is used with its symbolic name. For simplicity reasons, only the symbolic names are used.

Memory model
MIPS uses a classical memory model that can be used by the programmer. The upper memory address is 7FFFFFFFh (letter 'h' denotes a hexadecimal number). The memory is organized in areas as follows:

(a) code area (text) which hosts the program instructions
(b) data area (data) which hosts the data
(c) stack area (stack)

Instructions or/and pseudo-instructions of the symbolic language (Assembly)
The MIPS programming is achieved by using the available instructions ("normal" instructions or pseudo-instructions). The "normal" instructions are "translated" directly to machine language and the pseudo-instructions are "translated" to "normal" instructions for producing the final executable code. At code development level, the available instruction set contains "normal" as well as "pseudo" instructions. For simplicity reasons, the general term "instructions" will be used for all the instruction types.

Directives (or special commands) to the MIPS microprocessor (within the simulation environment)
These directives do not constitute instructions and are used for giving additional information for the program regarding the code and data areas, the text massages, etc.

Functions for specific program operations
Functions constitute complete subprograms that extend the main program functionality by offering useful operations such as keyboard reading, message displaying, etc.

Basic load instructions
```
li  Rdest,Src
```
#Load in Rdest an integer value or the content of another register
```
la Rdest,my_label
```
#Load the address of a label in Rdest
```
move Rdest,Rsrc
```
#Load a register from a register

Basic arithmetic (math) instructions
```
add Rdest,Rsrc1,Src
```
#Rdest=Rsrc1+Src
```
sub Rdest,Rsrc1,Src
```
#Rdest=Rsrc1-Src
```
mul Rdest,Rsrc1,Src
```
#Rdest=Rsrc1*Src
```
div Rdest,Rsrc1,Src
```
#Rdest=Rsrc1/Src

Control flow and branch-jump instructions
In Assembly language the corresponding implementation has the following logic:

```
if (condition-true) goto section LABEL
Instructions of the FALSE case
```

In the above implementation, if the condition is TRUE, then the execution flow is driven to section which starts from the point LABEL, otherwise (FALSE case) the following instructions (after the condition check) are executed.

The condition may involve a comparison with zero, any other number or the content of a register. These instructions start with the letter 'b' which is followed from two letters that denote the type of comparison and are completed with two or three arguments. If the comparison will be performed with zero, the following two arguments are used:

(a) register name (for comparing its content)
(b) label for branch-jump if the condition is TRUE

In the case of a register comparison with a register, the following three arguments are used:

(a) the name of the first register
(b) the name of the second register (or a number)
(c) label for branch-jump if the condition is TRUE

The smallest complete program

```
#Code section
.text 0x00400000

#Main program instructions

#Program termination (function 10)
li $v0,10
syscall

#Data section (optional)
.data

#Data declarations
```

Message form in the main memory
The ASCII codes of a message is stored within the main memory. Each message character occupies a memory location (1 byte). Through the instruction la, the starting address of the message is loaded in the desired register.

Conditional branches-jumps (changing the execution flow)
<u>Example</u>

```
bnez $t0, L1
```

In the above code, the content of $t0 is initially checked. if $t0 is not equal to 0 (TRUE case), then the execution flow is driven to L1, otherwise the execution flow is continued from the instruction bellow the condition-check (FALSE case).

Iteration loops
For developing iteration loops a condition-check has to be included in order to control (continue or stop) the iterations. The do-while loop is the most popular in Assembly language due to the fact that can be developed easily and corresponds directly to the C language instructions logic. The loop basic components such as the counter, the counter update and the condition-check are always needed independently of the language implementation (C or Assembly).

Answers and suggestions for the exercises with odd number

1.1

32

1.3

(a)

Symbol	Address	Content
msg	540A	'H'
msg+1	540B	'e'
msg+2	540C	'l'
msg+3	540D	'l'
msg+4	540E	'o'

(b)

$a0=540A

1.5

li $t0,12
add $t0,$t0,$t1
mul $t1,$t0,2
add $t0,$t0,$t1

1.7

(a)

mul $t1,$t1,2
div $t0,$t1,$t2

(b)

sub $t1,$t1,$t2
div $t1,$t0

(c)

mul $t2,$t2,$t2
mul $t0,$t1,$t3
mul $t0,$t0,4
sub $t0,$t2,$t0

(d)

sub $t0,$t1,$t2
mul $t4,$t4,3
mul $t0,$t0,$t4

1.9
```
li $v0,5
syscall
mov $a0,$v0
li $v0,1
syscall
```

1.11
```
mul $t1,$t1,2
mul $t2,$t2,$t2
mul $t2,$t2,$t2
mul $t2,$t2,2
div $t0,$t1,$t2
```

1.13
```
bne     $s3, $s4, L1
add     $s1, $s1, $s2
j               L2
L1:
add     $s1, $s1, $s1
L2:
```

1.15
Assume that $t0=i, $t1=x, $t2=y
```
i=x+y;
i=i-2;
x=x*y;
i=i+I;
```

1.17
```
la $a0,str      #Load the string starting address
li $v0,4        #Load the function number
syscall         #Function call
.data
str : .asciiz "Hello\n"
```

1.19
```
{
```

```
int i;
scanf("%d",&i);
}
```

1.21
```
li $t1,5
li $t2,4
add $t1,$t1,$t2
bne $t1,$t2,print
j exit
print:
        li $v0,1
        mov $a0,$t1
        syscall
exit:
```

1.23
2468101214161820

1.25
20

2 Developing basic MIPS Assembly Applications

Content-Goals

In this chapter the first applications using instructions, functions and programming structures will be developed. A main goal is to show that every program is based mainly on the available system functions.

Chapter Contents

2.1 Introduction

The applications that will be develop in this chapter are based on Assembly instructions, functions and programming structures in the most usual forms. The basic application categories include arithmetic operations and control as well as functions operations for supporting input (keyboard) and output (screen). In the next programs the framework with separated areas for code and data will be followed. The above separation is achieved by the corresponding directives. Finally, it has to be mentioned that all the applications follow a progressive difficulty in order to achieve the needed knowledge gain by the reader.

2.2 Applications development

2.2.1 Instruction sequence – System functions – Basic arithmetic operations

Application 1 – Message display

This application displays a message on the screen (console window within the simulator). Despite the application simplicity the first function usage is presented. The application program displays a message and then is terminated.

As will be shown, the program includes a data section for declaring the message as well as a code section for displaying the message through the print_string function.

Figure 2.1 shows the flow chart and the corresponding code.

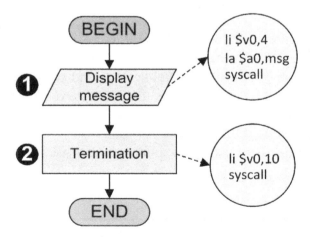

Figure 2.1 Flow chart for displaying a message

Code development

As shown in figure 2.1, the program consists only of two functions. The programmer does not develop his own code.

```
.text 0x00400000
```

Initially, the starting address of the code section is declared (0x00400000). This address is derived from the memory model of the MIPS microprocessor.

```
li $v0,4
la $a0,msg
syscall
```

Next, the message is displayed on the screen through the function 4. As mentioned in previous chapter, for displaying an alphanumeric (string), the starting address of the message within the memory has to be set. This is achieved through the message label which corresponds to a real memory address.

```
li $v0,10
syscall
```

The program termination is performed through the function 10 which has no arguments. This function requires the minimum code (in $v0 the function number) and finally the syscall instruction which is placed always after the argument preparation. Note also that the argument preparation sequence does not play any role.

```
.data
msg: .asciiz "My first program \n"
```

This is the starting point of the data area and the message declaration. Note that in the message declaration the directive .asciiz is used instead of

.ascii for placing utomatically the termination character. Additionally, the character "\n" is used for changing the line.

The complete code is following.

```
#Application 1
.text 0x00400000        #Code section

                        #Using function 4 (Display message)
li $v0,4                #Load the function number
la $a0,msg              #Load the message starting address
syscall                 #Function call

                        #Using function 10 (Termination)
li $v0,10               #Load the function number
syscall                 #Function call

.data                   #Data section
msg: .asciiz "My first program \n"
```

Application 2 – Read and display numbers

The functions for read and display, support the most important program operations for parameterization and result printing. The above functions are used always with the same way.

(a) Reading and displaying a number

The first program reads a number from the keyboard and then this number is displayed on the screen.

Figure 2.2 shows the algorithmic structure as well as the corresponding functions at code level. The function 4 is used two times for displaying help messages. The only difference is the corresponding label of the message. The code structure is sequential and that means that the instructions are executed in turn.

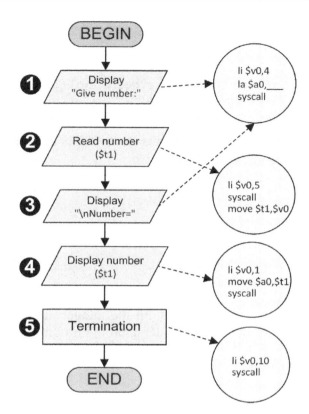

Figure 2.2 Flow chart for reading and displaying a number

Code development

```
text 0x00400000
```
Code section

```
li $v0,4
la $a0,msg_read_int
syscall
```

Display a help message before the read of the integer number from the keyboard. Without this message the user does not know what to enter.

```
li $v0,5
```

```
syscall
move $t1,$v0
```

An integer number is read from the keyboard through the function 5. The number is automatically stored in $v0 (by the function). After that, the number is temporarily stored in $t1. The next code uses also the $v0 (instruction li $v0,value) and thus its contents are lost. The previous content of $v0 is already stored in $t1.

```
li $v0,4
la $a0,msg_print_int
syscall
```

Display a help message before displaying the integer number on the screen. This is done for helping the user to understand the program operation.

```
li $v0,1
move $a0,$t1
syscall
```

The number display is performed through the function 1 (the number has to be stored in $a0). Note that the number to be displayed is initially stored in $t1 (after the use of function 5).

```
li $v0,10
syscall
```

The program is terminated normally through the function 10 which does not have any argument.

```
.data
msg_read_int:           .asciiz "Give number:"
```

```
msg_print_int:        .asciiz "\nNumber="
```

The program data include the two messages. These messages are declared with the same directive. The complete code is following.

#Application 2(a)

```
.text 0x00400000      #Code section

                      #Display the message "Give number:"
li $v0,4              #Load the function number
la $a0,msg_read_int   #Load the message starting address
syscall               #Function call

                      #Read number (keyboard)
li $v0,5              #Load the function number
syscall               #Function call
move $t1,$v0          #Store the number in $t1

                      #Display "\nNumber="
li $v0,4              #Load the function number
la $a0,msg_print_int  #Load the message starting address
syscall               #Function call

                      #Display number (Screen)
li $v0,1              #Load the function number
move $a0,$t1          #Load the number to be displayed in $a0
syscall               #Function call

li $v0,10             #Program termination
syscall               #Function call

.data                 #Data section
msg_read_int:  .asciiz "Give number:"
msg_print_int: .asciiz "\nNumber="
```

(b) Reading and displaying three numbers

This program reads and displays three numbers but does not have any significant differences as compared to previous program (the same functions are used more times). The flow chart of figure 2.3 shows the sequence of functions usage in order to implement the program operation.

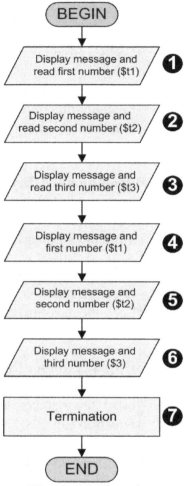

Figure 2.3 Flow chart

Code development

```
.text 0x00400000
```

Code start

```
li $v0,4
la $a0,read_a
syscall
```

Display a help message before reading the first number. In this application, three numbers are read and thus the help messages are strongly needed.

```
li $v0,5
syscall
move $t1,$v0
```

Read the first number from keyboard and store the number from $v0 to $t1 because the $v0 is needed in the next instruction.

```
li $v0,4
la $a0,read_b
syscall
```

Display a help message before reading the second number. Note that the three instructions for the function 4 are copied from the previous paragraph with the only difference the message label.

```
li $v0,5
syscall
move $t2,$v0
```

Next, the second number is read from the keyboard. In this case, the function 5 has been copied from the previous paragraph. The only difference is the register where the integer number is stored.

```
li $v0,4
la $a0,read_c
syscall
```

Display a help message (like previously) before reading the number.

```
li $v0,5
syscall
move $t3,$v0
```

The code section for reading the three numbers is now completed by reading the third number. For simplicity reasons the three numbers have been stored in the registers $t1,$t2 and $t3 respectively.

```
li $v0,4
la $a0,print_a
syscall
```

Display a help message before displaying the first number. This message is helpful for separating the numbers on screen.

```
li $v0,1
move $a0,$t1
syscall
```

Display the first number (the first number is stored in $t1).

```
li $v0,4
la $a0,print_b
syscall
```

Next, another help message is displayed before displaying the second number. Please note how the same code is repeated. This feature, denotes the code simplicity.

```
li $v0,1
move $a0,$t2
syscall
```

Display the second number which is stored in $t2. For displaying an integer number, always the function 1 is used.

```
li $v0,4
la $a0,print_c
syscall
```

The program is completed with displaying the third number.

```
li $v0,1
move $a0,$t3
syscall
```

Display the third number which is stored in $t3.

```
li $v0,10
syscall
```

Program termination with function 10.

```
.data       #Data section
read_a:    .asciiz "Give number A:"
read_b:    .asciiz "Give number B:"
read_c:    .asciiz "Give number C:"
print_a:   .asciiz "\nNumber A="
```

```
print_b:    .asciiz "\nNumber B="
print_c:    .asciiz "\nNumber C="
```

The data section includes the program messages that are displayed through function 4 (within the code section).

The complete code is following.

#Application 2(b)

```
.text 0x00400000        #Code section

                        #Display the message "Give number A:"
li $v0,4                #Load the function number
la $a0,read_a           #Load the message starting address
syscall                 #Function call

                        #Read the first number
li $v0,5                #Load the function number
syscall                 #Function call
move $t1,$v0            #Load the first number in $t1

                        #Display the message "Give number B:"
li $v0,4                #Load the function number
la $a0,read_b           #Load the message starting address
syscall                 #Function call

                        #Read the second number
li $v0,5                #Load the function number
syscall                 #Function call
move $t2,$v0            #Load the second number in $t2

                        #Display the message "Give number C:"
li $v0,4                #Load the function number
la $a0,read_c           #Load the message starting address
syscall                 #Function call

                        #Read the third number
li $v0,5                #Load the function number
syscall                 #Function call
move $t3,$v0            #Load the third number in $t3
```

```
                          #Display the message "\nNumber A="
li $v0,4                  #Load the function number
la $a0,print_a            #Load the message starting address
syscall                   #Function call

                          #Display the first number
li $v0,1                  #Load the function number
move $a0,$t1              #Load the first number to be displayed
syscall                   #Function call

                          #Display the message "\nNumber B="
li $v0,4                  #Load the function number
la $a0,print_b            #Load the message starting address
syscall                   #Function call

                          #Display the second number
li $v0,1                  #Load the function number
move $a0,$t2              #Load the second number to be displayed
syscall                   #Function call

                          #Display the message "\nNumber C="
li $v0,4                  #Load the function number
la $a0,print_c            #Load the message starting address
syscall                   #Function call

                          #Display the third number
li $v0,1                  #Load the function number
move $a0,$t3              #Load the third number to be displayed
syscall                   #Function call

                          #Program termination
li $v0,10                 #Load the function number
syscall                   #Function call

.data                     #Data section
read_a:    .asciiz "Give number A:"
read_b:    .asciiz "Give number B:"
read_c:    .asciiz "Give number C:"
print_a:   .asciiz "\nNumber A="
```

```
print_b:    .asciiz "\nNumber B="
print_c:    .asciiz "\nNumber C="
```

Application 3 – Arithmetic calculations

Arithmetic calculations are important operations that are used in the most of the programs. The available MIPS instructions support only the four basic arithmetic operations (addition, subtraction, multiplication, division) between two arguments. That means that a more complex arithmetic expression has to be separated in simpler operations in order to be performed by the available MIPS instructions. The next program implements the following calculations:

(a) X1=A-B-C
(b) X2=A+B-(C/2)
(c) X3=(3*A)+(B*C)

Obviously, there is no instruction to implement the above expressions-calculations directly. Thus, for every calculation the proper MIPS arithmetic instructions have to be combined. Please note that the above operations are based on the integer arithmetic and only the integer part of a result is kept.

For simplicity reasons it is assumed that the numbers A, B and C, are represented by the registers $t1, $t2 and $t3 respectively. Additionally, X1, X2 and X3 are represented by other available registers. This program is similar with the previous and thus a flow chart is not necessary.

Code development

```
.text 0x00400000
```

Code section from the address 0x00400000.

```
li $v0,5
syscall
move $t1,$v0
```

Read the first integer number. This program does not display any help message before the number read. The first number is stored in $t1 through the instruction move.

```
li $v0,5
syscall
move $t2,$v0
```

Read the second number and store the value in $t2 (number B).

```
li $v0,5
syscall
move $t3,$v0
```

Read the third number (number C).

```
sub $t0,$t1,$t2
sub $t0,$t0,$t3
```

The above code implements the expression X1=A-B-C. Initially the A-B ($t1-$t2) is calculated and the result is stored in $t0. Next, the register $t3 (number C) is subtracted from $t0 which already contains the A-B. Finally, the A-B-C is calculated.

```
li $v0,4
la $a0,x1
syscall
```

Before display the first result, a help message is displayed for denoting that the result is for X1.

```
li $v0,1
move $a0,$t0
syscall
```

Before the next calculation, the above result is displayed (using the function 1).

```
add $t0,$t1,$t2
div $t4,$t3,2
sub $t0,$t0,$t4
```

The above calculation is for X2=A+B-(C/2). The partial calculations can be performed in any order but the (C/2) has to be taken in account as a single number. The calculation can be started from A+B ($t1+$t2), while the result is stored in $t0. Next, the division is calculated and then the final subtraction. Remember that the arithmetic operation is perform firstly between the second and third argument and the result is stored in the first argument.

```
li $v0,4
la $a0,x2
syscall
```

Display a help message before displaying the X2.

```
li $v0,1
move $a0,$t0
syscall
```

The result is displayed again with the function 1. The X2 is initially loaded in $a0 for using the function 1.

```
mul $t0,$t1,3
mul $t1,$t2,$t3
add $t0,$t0,$t1
```

The last calculation is X3=(3*A)+(B*C). Initially, the products are calculated (multiplication) and then the addition. Remember that only one arithmetic operation between two arguments can be performed at a time.

```
li $v0,4
la $a0,x3
syscall
```

Display a help message before the third calculation.
```
li $v0,1
move $a0,$t0
syscall
```

Display the last result (X3) with function 1.

```
li $v0,10
syscall
```

Program termination

```
.data
x1: .asciiz "\nX1="
x2: .asciiz "\nX2="
x3: .asciiz "\nX3="
```

The data area includes only the help messages for displaying the results. Note also, that just after each calculation the corresponding result is displayed. In other words the calculations are not performed in the same group of code. This is done especially when there are not enough free registers. On the other hand, the grouping of arithmetic operations is a choice of the programmer. In real programming, the main memory is used for managing and performing calculations with many numbers and thus all the available addressing methods have to be known.
The complete code is following.

#Application 3

`.text 0x00400000`	**#Code section**
	#Read the first number (A)
`li $v0,5`	#Load the function number
`syscall`	#Function call
`move $t1,$v0`	#Load the first number in $t1
	#Read the second number (B)
`li $v0,5`	#Load the function number
`syscall`	#Function call
`move $t2,$v0`	#Load the second number in $t2
	#Read the third number (C)
`li $v0,5`	#Load the function number
`syscall`	#Function call
`move $t3,$v0`	#Load the third number in $t3

```
                        #Calculate X1=A-B-C
sub $t0,$t1,$t2         #$t0=$t1-$t2, (A-B)
sub $t0,$t0,$t3         #$t0=$t0-$t3, ((A-B)-C)


                        #Display message "\nX1="
li $v0,4                #Load the function number
la $a0,x1               #Load the message starting address
syscall                 #Function call


                        #Display result X1
li $v0,1                #Load the function number
move $a0,$t0            #Load the result to be displayed
syscall                 #Function call


                        #Calculate X2=A+B-(C/2)
add $t0,$t1,$t2         #$t0=$t1+$t2, (A+B)
div $t4,$t3,2           #$t4=$t3/2, (C/2)
sub $t0,$t0,$t4         #$t0=$t0-$t4, ((A+B)-(C/2))


                        #Display message "\nX2="
li $v0,4                #Load the function number
la $a0,x2               #Load the message starting address
syscall                 #Function call


                        #Display result X2
li $v0,1                #Load the function number
move $a0,$t0            #Load the result to be displayed
syscall                 #Function call


                        #Calculate X3=(3*A)+(B*C)
mul $t0,$t1,3           #$t0=$t1*3, A*3
mul $t1,$t2,$t3         #$t1=$t2*$t3, B*C
add $t0,$t0,$t1         #$t0=$t0+$t1, (A*3)+(B*C)


                        #Display message "\nX3="
li $v0,4                #Load the function number
la $a0,x3               #Load the message starting address
syscall                 #Function call
```

```
                        #Display result X3
li $v0,1                #Load the function number
move $a0,$t0            #Load the result to be displayed
syscall                 #Function call

                        #Program termination
li $v0,10               #Load the function number
syscall                 #Function call

.data                   #Data section
x1: .asciiz "\nX1="
x2: .asciiz "\nX2="
x3: .asciiz "\nX3="
```

Application 4 – Parameterized result display

Until now, only "constant" messages are displayed in the applications. In other words, a message is always displayed in the same form. In some cases the messages have to be adapted according to the results. If for example the message "(3*A)+(B*C)" is declared, then will be always displayed in this form independently of the values of A and B. In this application the characters 'A', 'B', and 'C' will be replaced by the corresponding values. Assuming that A=2, B=1 and C=3, the message will be displayed in the form x3=(3*2)+(1*3)=9. Now, the message consists of constant and variable parts. Thus, the message will be displayed using a combination of the functions 4 and 1 respectively.

Figure 2.4 shows the message components as well as the needed functions for the corresponding displaying.

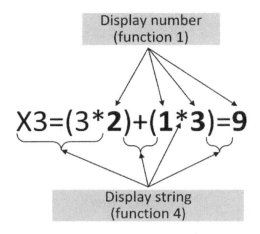

Display number
(function 1)

$$X3=(3*2)+(1*3)=9$$

Display string
(function 4)

Figure 2.4 Message form

The needed functions in order to display the message of figure 2.4, are placed in the program in specific order. In the above message the numbers 2, 1 and 3 are numerical data and will be used for the arithmetic calculations. Inside the code, the functions will be placed in the following order:

(1) Function 4 (Display "X3=(3*")
(2) Function 1 (Display the number 2 which has entered from the keyboard and represents A)
(3) Function 4 (Display ")+(")
(4) Function 1 (Display the number 1 which has entered from the keyboard and represents B)
(5) Function 4 (Display "*")
(6) Function 1 (Display the number 3 which has entered from the keyboard and represents C)
(7) Function 4 (Display ")=")
(8) Function 1 (Display result)

At code level, the message display will be performed as follows:

```
li $v0,4
la $a0,m1
syscall
```

   #Display the message "x3=(3*"

```
li $v0,1
move $a0,$t1              #Display the first number
syscall
```

②

```
li $v0,4
la $a0,m2                #Display the message ")+("
syscall
```

③

```
li $v0,1
move $a0,$t2             #Display the second number
syscall
```

④

```
li $v0,4
la $a0,m3                #Display the message "*"
syscall
```

⑤

```
li $v0,1
move $a0,$t3             #Display the third number
syscall
```

⑥

```
li $v0,4
la $a0,m4                #Display the message ")="
syscall
```

⑦

```
li $v0,1
move $a0,$t0             #Display the result
syscall
```

⑧

Complete code development

```
.text 0x00400000
```

Code section

```
li $v0,5
syscall
move $t1,$v0
```

Read the first integer number (number A). Store the number in $t1

```
li $v0,5
syscall
move $t2,$v0
```

Read the first integer number (number B). Store the number in $t2

```
li $v0,5
syscall
move $t3,$v0
```

Read the first integer number (number C). Store the number in $t3

```
mul $t0,$t1,3
mul $t4,$t2,$t3
add $t0,$t0,$t4
```

Arithmetic calculation. Initially the 3*A is calculated. Next the B*C is calculated and finally the (3*A)+(B*C)

```
li $v0,4
la $a0,m1
syscall
```

Display the first part of the message (string)

```
li $v0,1
move $a0,$t1
syscall
```

Display number A

```
li $v0,4
la $a0,m2
syscall
```

Display string after the number A

```
li $v0,1
move $a0,$t2
syscall
```

Display the second number (B)

```
li $v0,4
la $a0,m3
syscall
```

Display "*" that follows the number B

```
li $v0,1
move $a0,$t3
syscall
```

Display the third number

```
li $v0,4
la $a0,m4
syscall
```

Display the rest string before the arithmetic result

```
li $v0,1
move $a0,$t0
syscall
```

Display the arithmetic result

```
li $v0,10
syscall
```
Program termination with function 10

```
.data
m1: .asciiz "x3=(3*"
m2: .asciiz ")+("
m3: .asciiz "*"
```

```
m4: .asciiz ")="
```

Messages (strings) declarations.

The complete code is following.

```
#Application 4
.text 0x00400000        #Code section

                        #Read the first number
li $v0,5                #Load the function number
syscall                 #Function call
move $t1,$v0            #Load the first number in $t1

                        #Read the second number
li $v0,5                #Load the function number
syscall                 #Function call
move $t2,$v0            #Load the first number in $t2

                        #Read the third number
li $v0,5                #Load the function number
syscall                 #Function call
move $t3,$v0            #Load the first number in $t3


                        #Calculate X3=(3*A)+(B*C)
mul $t0,$t1,3           #$t0=$t1*3, (A*3)
mul $t4,$t2,$t3         #$t4=$t2*$t3, (B*C)
add $t0,$t0,$t4         #$t0=$t0+$t4, (A*3)+(B*C)

                        #Display the message "x3=(3*"
li $v0,4                #Load the function number
la $a0,m1               #Load the message starting address
syscall                 #Function call

                        #Display the first number
li $v0,1                #Load the function number
move $a0,$t1            #Load the first number to be displayed
syscall                 #Function call
```

```
                              #Display the message ")+("
li $v0,4                      #Load the function number
la $a0,m2                     #Load the message starting address
syscall                       #Function call

                              #Display the second number
li $v0,1                      #Load the function number
move $a0,$t2                  #Load the second number to be displayed
syscall                       #Function call

                              #Display the message "*"
li $v0,4                      #Load the function number
la $a0,m3                     #Load the message starting address
syscall                       #Function call

                              #Display the third number
li $v0,1                      #Load the function number
move $a0,$t3                  #Load the third number to be displayed
syscall                       #Function call

                              #Display the message ")="
li $v0,4                      #Load the function number
la $a0,m4                     #Load the message starting address
syscall                       #Function call

                              #Display result
li $v0,1                      #Load the function number
move $a0,$t0                  #Load the result to be displayed
syscall                       #Function call

                              #Program termination
li $v0,10                     #Load the function number
syscall                       #Function call

.data                         #Data section
m1: .asciiz "x3=(3*"
m2: .asciiz ")+("
m3: .asciiz "*"
m4: .asciiz ")="
```

Application 5 - Parameterized result display with memory management

As presented in the previous application, the combination of strings and numbers in one message is a difficult situation. Thus, an alternative and more effective method has to be investigated. In this application the same message as previously will be displayed by using only one string inside the data section. The question here is how the numerical data can be inserted within the message by using only once the function 4. The corresponding message will be declared as follows:

```
m1:  .asciiz "x3=(3*X)+(X*X)="
```

If the function 4 is used directly, then the message will be displayed as is. The function 4 will be used as follows:

```
li $v0,4
la $a0,m1
syscall
```

The main point is to replace "X"s with the numbers that are entered from the keyboard. Initially the "X"s memory locations have to be accessed.

Assuming that the message starts in address m1, the first character is located in the address m1+0, the first "X" character in the address m1+6, the second "X" character in the address m1+10 (m1+A in hexadecimal) and the third "X" in the address m1+12 (m1+C in hexadecimal). Thus, if the proper numbers are placed in the above memory locations, then the message will be displayed in the required form. Figure 2.5 shows the message within the main memory and the corresponding locations for placing the numbers. Note that in the above memory locations the "X" characters have been selected randomly and will be replaced through the program code.

The MIPS simulator displays only ASCII characters. It is assumed that in every memory location, the ASCII code of the message characters is stored. For simplicity reasons, figure 2.5 shows the corresponding characters (within quotation marks) and not the ASCII codes. As mentioned before, the addresses m1+6, m1+A and m1+C have to be accessed in order the corresponding numbers to be placed. If the numbers are placed directly to the above memory locations, then nothing will be displayed on screen. If for example the number 1 is entered, then the system will try to display the character with ASCII code 1 which does not correspond to "1" (printable character). Thus the entered number has to be converted to ASCII character.

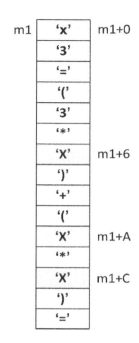

Figure 2.5
Message inside memory

This is achieved by adding in the number 1 the number 30h in hexadecimal or 48 in decimal. Due to the fact that the characters '0', '1', '2' to '9' have ASCII codes 30h, 31h, 32h to 39h (in hexadecimal) respectively, if the number 30h is added to 1, then the resulted number is 31h which corresponds to the ASCII character '1'. Thus, the numbers conversion to characters has to be performed before the storage in the main memory. Note also that the above approach works only with single digit numbers. If a number has more than one digits, then all the digits have to be converted separately and the corresponding memory has to be formed in the proper way.

Assume now that the first number is 1. As mentioned before, the number will be initially converted in ASCII code and then will be stored in the address m1+6. With an add instruction the 48 (30h in hexadecimal) is added to the above number (it is assumed that the number is stored in $t1). Moreover the value 6 has to be loaded in a register for producing the deviation from the memory location m1.

```
li $t5,6
add $t1,$t1,48
```

With the above instructions, the register $t5 contains the deviation from the address m1, while $t1 contains the ASCII code of the character "1". The next step is to store the ASCII code within the message (memory area) for displaying the message correctly using the function 4. For storing the ASCII code, a store instruction will be used (available instructions sw, sh, sb). Despite the fact that every register has a capacity of 32bits (4 bytes), only 8bits are required for the ASCII code and thus the instruction sb will be used. The sb instruction will store the least significant byte of the register inside the memory.

```
sb $t1,m1($t5)
```

Thus, the content of $t1 (ASCII code) will be stored in the memory address m1+$t5 (i.e. m1+6). Figure 2.6 shows how the conversion to ASCII code and the storage in memory are achieved. Based on figure 2.6, every instruction group performs the following operations:

(a) Update the deviation register ($t5)
(b) Convert to ASCII code (addition of the number 48, i.e. 30h in hexadecimal)
(c) Store the ASCII code (character) inside memory (message area)

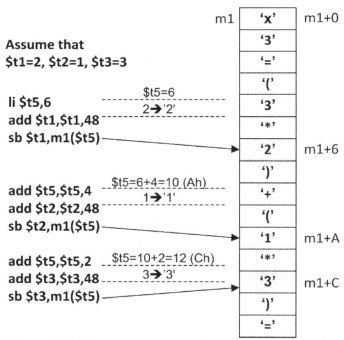

Figure 2.6 Memory access and message preparation

Code development

```
.text 0x00400000
```

Code section

```
li $v0,5
syscall
move $t1,$v0
```

Load the first number

```
li $v0,5
syscall
move $t2,$v0
```

Load the second number

```
li $v0,5
syscall
move $t3,$v0
```

Load the third number

```
mul $t0,$t1,3
mul $t4,$t2,$t3
add $t0,$t0,$t4
```

Calculation of (3*A)+(B*C). The result is just a number and thus it will be displayed directly with the function 1.

```
li $t5,6
add $t1,$t1,48
sb $t1,m1($t5)
```

Store the first number (in ASCII form) in the memory. Initially, the number 6 is defined as the first deviation. Next the first number ($t1) is converted to ASCII code. Finally the resulted character is stored in the address m1+6.

```
add $t5,$t5,4
```

```
add $t2,$t2,48
sb $t2,m1($t5)
```

The next step is to store the second number inside the message using the previous approach. The deviation is increased by 4. Thus the new storage takes place in the address m1+10.

```
add $t5,$t5,2
add $t3,$t3,48
sb $t3,m1($t5)
```

The message access is completed with the storage of the third number in the address m1+12.

```
li $v0,4
la $a0,m1
syscall
```

After the previous operations, the message for the required calculation is ready for display using the function 4.

```
li $v0,1
move $a0,$t0
syscall
```

The final result is displayed before the program termination

```
li $v0,10
syscall
```

Program termination

```
.data
m1:  .asciiz "x3=(3*X)+(X*X)="
```

Message in the data area

The complete code is following.

#Application 5

```
.text 0x00400000        #Code section
```

#Read the first number

```
li $v0,5                #Load the function number
syscall                 #Function call
move $t1,$v0            #Load the first number in $t1
```

#Read the second number

```
li $v0,5                #Load the function number
syscall                 #Function call
move $t2,$v0            #Load the first number in $t2
```

#Read the third number

```
li $v0,5                #Load the function number
syscall                 #Function call
move $t3,$v0            #Load the first number in $t3
```

#Calculation of X3=(3*A)+(B*C)

```
mul $t0,$t1,3           #$t0=$t1*3, (A*3)
mul $t4,$t2,$t3         #$t4=$t2*$t3, (B*C)
add $t0,$t0,$t4         #$t0=$t0+$t4, (A*3)+(B*C)
```

```
                        #Convert to ASCII the first (one digit)
                        #number (A) and store the result
                        #in the memory (inside message)
li $t5,6                #Deviation from the message
                        #starting address
add $t1,$t1,48          #Convert to ASCII code
sb $t1,m1($t5)          #Store the ASCII code in m1+$t5 (m1+6)
```

```
add $t5,$t5,4           #Deviation from the message start
add $t2,$t2,48          #Convert to ASCII code
sb $t2,m1($t5)          #Store the ASCII code in m1+$t5 (m1+6+4)
```

```
add $t5,$t5,2           #Deviation from the message start
add $t3,$t3,48          #Convert to ASCII code
sb $t3,m1($t5)          #Store the ASCII
                        #code in m1+$t5 (m1+6+4+2)
```

#Display the final message
```
li $v0,4          #Load the function number
la $a0,m1         #Load the message starting address
syscall           #Function call
```

#Display result
```
li $v0,1          #Load the function number
move $a0,$t0      #Load the result to be displayed
syscall           #Function call
```

#Program termination
```
li $v0,10         #Load the function number
syscall           #Function call
```

```
.data             #Data section
m1: .asciiz "x3=(3*X)+(X*X)="
```

2.2.2 Control-Repetition-Calculations

Application 6 – Checking for positive, negative or zero number

In this application, condition-check and branch instructions are used. More precisely, a number will be checked if is it positive, negative or zero. In such a case only two condition checks are needed. If the two first conditions are FALSE, then the third case is TRUE. Figure 2.7 shows the algorithm for the conditions-checks and the corresponding messages display. Initially, a number is entered from the keyboard. If the number is positive (TRUE case), then the corresponding message is displayed. Otherwise (FALSE case) the case of a negative number is checked. If the number is negative (TRUE case of the condition check), then the corresponding message is displayed, otherwise (FALSE case) the number is zero (the two previous cases have already rejected).

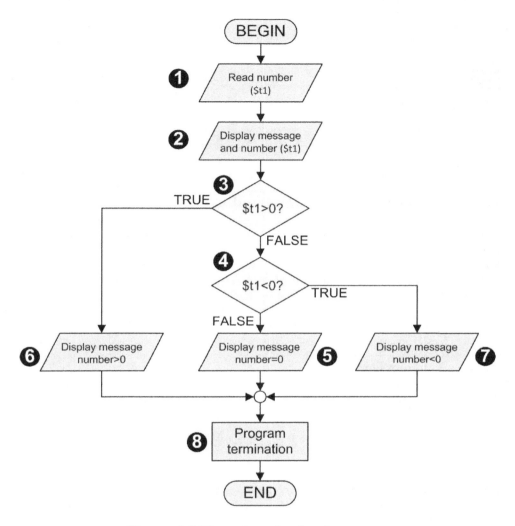

Figure 2.7 Flow chart for the three cases

Code development
The following code implements the algorithm of figure 2.7.

```
.text 0x00400000
```

Code section

```
li $v0,5
syscall
move $t1,$v0
```

Read an integer number from the keyboard and store in $t1.

```
li $v0,4
la $a0,arith
syscall
```

Display a help message

```
li $v0,1
move $a0,$t1
syscall
```

Display the integer number

```
bgtz $t1,mega
```

If the number in $t1 is greater than zero, then the execution flow is driven to the label mega.

```
bltz $t1,mikr
```

If the number in $t1 is less than zero, then the execution flow is driven to the label mikr. This condition check is performed only if the previous condition-check is FALSE.

```
li $v0,4
la $a0,miden_msg
syscall
```

Display the message that the number in $t1 is zero. The execution flow reaches this point if no one of the above conditions-checks is TRUE (thus the third case is TRUE).

```
j exodos
```

Jump to the label exodos for avoiding the next instructions that belong to other cases.

```
mega:
```

```
li $v0,4
la $a0,meg_msg
syscall
```

Display the message that the number in $t1 is greater than zero

```
j exodos
```

Jump to the label exodos

```
mikr:
```

```
li $v0,4
la $a0,mik_msg
syscall
```

Display the message that the number in `$t1` is less than zero. At this point a jump instruction to label `exodos` does not make sense. Is a wrong programming technique to put here a jump instruction to `exodos` because the execution flow will be driven to that label anyway.

Remember that a label is not an instruction and does not change the execution flow.

```
exodos:
     li $v0,10
     syscall
```

Program termination with the function 10.

```
.data

meg_msg:    .asciiz "\nNumber>0"
mik_msg:    .asciiz "\nNumber<0"
miden_msg:  .asciiz "\nNumber=0"
arith:      .asciiz "\nNumber="
```

Messages declarations in the data section.

The complete code is following.

#Application 6

```
.text 0x00400000      #Code section

                      #Read number
li $v0,5              #Load the function number
syscall               #Function call
move $t1,$v0          #Load the number in $t1

                      #Display the message "\nNumber="
```

```
li $v0,4                  #Load the function number
la $a0,arith              #Load the message starting address
syscall                   #Function call
```

#Display number
```
li $v0,1                  #Load the function number
move $a0,$t1              #Load the number to be displayed
syscall                   #Function call
```

#Check number
```
bgtz $t1,mega             #If $t1>0, then goto mega
bltz $t1,mikr             #If $t1<0, then goto mikr
```

#$t1=0
#Display the message "\nNumber=0"
```
li $v0,4                  #Load the function number
la $a0,miden_msg          #Load the message starting address
syscall                   #Function call
```

```
j exodos                  #Goto to program termination
```

```
mega:                     #Code for $t1>0
```
#Code for $t1>0
```
                          #Display the message "\nNumber>0"
    li $v0,4              #Load the function number
    la $a0,meg_msg       #Load the message starting address
    syscall              #Function call
```

```
    j exodos             #Goto program termination
```

```
mikr:                     #Code for $t1<0
```
#Code for $t1<0
```
                          #Display the message "\nNumber<0"
    li $v0,4             #Load the function number
    la $a0,mik_msg      #Load the message starting address
    syscall             #Function call
```

```
exodos:                   #Program termination
```
#Program termination
```
    li $v0,10            #Load the function number
    syscall             #Function call
```

```
.data                           #Data section

meg_msg:    .asciiz  "\nNumber>0"
mik_msg:    .asciiz  "\n<Number0"
miden_msg:.asciiz  "\nNumber=0"
arith:      .asciiz  "\nNumber="
```

Application 7 – Checking a value range and calculation

A usual condition-check is if a number belongs to a value range. A number belongs to a value range if two conditions-checks are TRUE simultaneously. The first check is for the left limit and the second check is for the right limit. The check can be implemented with two different ways. Assuming that the value range is [A,B], the check can be implemented as follows:

First approach
If the number is greater or equal to A AND less or equal to B, then the number belongs to the value range, otherwise does not belong.

Second approach
If the number is less than A OR greater than B, then the number does not belong to the value range, otherwise belongs.

In this application the second approach has been chosen for simplicity reasons. Moreover, every time a number is entered and does not belong to that value range then the execution flow is driven back to start for reading again the number. Finally, if the number belongs to that value range then the square is calculated.

Figure 2.8 shows the corresponding flow chart.

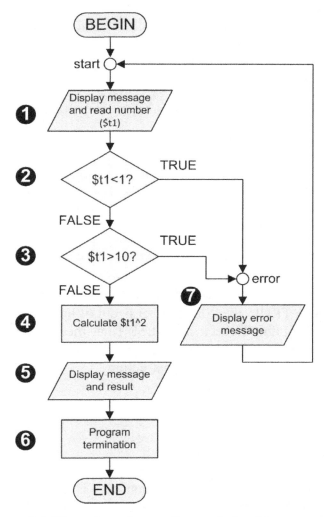

Figure 2.8 Flow chart for reading and checking a number

Code development

```
.text 0x00400000
```

Code section

```
start:
      li $v0,4
```

```
la $a0,read_int
syscall

li $v0,5
syscall
move $t1,$v0
```

Display a help message (function 4) and read an integer number (function 5) from keyboard.

```
blt $t1,1,error
```

If $t1 is less than 1, then the execution flow is driven to error (if the condition-check is TRUE, then the number is out of the value range from the left side). If the condition-check is FALSE (that means that the number is greater or equal to 1), the execution flow is not driven to error and the execution is continued from the next instruction.

```
bgt $t1,10,error
```

If $t1 is greater than 10, then the execution flow is driven to error (if the condition-check is TRUE, then the number is out of the value range from the right side). If the condition-check is FALSE (that means that the number is less or equal to 10), the execution flow is not driven to error and the execution is continued from the next instruction. Practically this means that the number finally belongs to that range.

```
mul $t1,$t1,$t1
```

Calculating the square of the number (previously has been checked that belongs to the value range). With this instruction the register $t1 is multiplied with its self and the result is stored again in $t1.

```
li $v0,4
la $a0,apot
syscall

li $v0,1
move $a0,$t1
syscall
```

Display a help message (function 4) and the arithmetic result (function 1).

```
exodos:
    li $v0,10
    syscall
```

Program termination

```
error:
    li $v0,4
    la $a0,error_msg
    syscall
    jstart
```

Display the error message (function 4) and return to start (label start) for reading the integer number from the keyboard.

```
.data
error_msg:  .asciiz "\nERROR! Out of range [1,10]"
apot:       .asciiz "\nX^2="
read_int:   .asciiz "\nGive Number:"
```

Data section with messages

The complete code is following.

```
#Application 7
.text 0x00400000                    #Code section

start:                              #Display the message "\nGive Number:"
    li $v0,4                        #Load the function number
    la $a0,read_int                 #Load the message starting address
    syscall                         #Function call

                                    #Read the number
    li $v0,5                        #Load the function number
    syscall                         #Function call
    move $t1,$v0                    #Load the number in $t1

    blt $t1,1,error                 #Out of range from the left side,
                                    #Goto error
    bgt $t1,10,error                #Out of range from the right side,
                                    #Goto error

                                    #The number belongs to value range
    mul $t1,$t1,$t1                 #Square calculation ($t1=$t1*$t1)

                                    #Display the message "\nX^2="
    li $v0,4                        #Load the function number
    la $a0,apot                     #Load the message starting address
    syscall                         #Function call

                                    #Display result
    li $v0,1                        #Load the function number
    move $a0,$t1                    #Load the result to be displayed
    syscall                         #Function call

exodos:                             #Program termination
    li $v0,10                       #Load the function number
    syscall                         #Function call
```

```
error:                          #Display the message "\n ERROR!
                                #Out of range [1,10]"
    li $v0,4                    #Load the function number
    la $a0,error_msg           #Load the message starting address
    syscall                    #Function call
    j start                    #return to start, read new number


.data                           #Data section


error_msg: .asciiz "\n ERROR! Out of range [1,10]"
apot:      .asciiz "\nX^2="
read_int:  .asciiz "\nGive Number:"
```

Application 8 – Finding values that make zero an arithmetic calculation

In many applications, various arithmetic calculations in functions and expressions are performed. In some cases the values that make zero a function are calculated. The programming approach is more effective than the mathematical analysis. Based on the above approach an iteration loop is used in order to test a value range that makes the function zero (finding a zero result). This is very useful especially when the value that makes zero a denominator has to be found for avoiding division by zero.

In this application, the function coefficients as well as the value range to be tested are entered. More precisely, the value of function $f(x)=ax^2+bx$, with x in the value range [X1,X2] is calculated. The a and b coefficients as well as the limits (X1, X2) of the value range are entered from the keyboard. Figure 2.9 shows the corresponding flow chart.

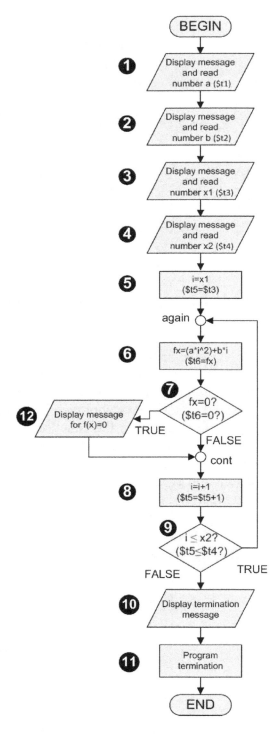

Figure 2.9 Flow chart for the function f(x)

Code development

```
.text 0x00400000
```

Code section

```
start:
    li $v0,4
    la $a0,read_a
    syscall


    li $v0,5
    syscall
    move $t1,$v0
```

Initially a help message is displayed and the a coefficient is entered from the keyboard.

```
    li $v0,4
    la $a0,read_b
    syscall

    li $v0,5
    syscall
    move $t2,$v0
```

Next the b coefficient is entered after the help message display.

```
    li $v0,4
```

```
        la $a0,range
        syscall

        li $v0,4
        la $a0,read_x1
        syscall

        li $v0,5
        syscall
        move $t3,$v0
```

Display (function 4) a help message for the value range and the left limit. Then, the left limit is entered (function 5) from the keyboard.

```
        li $v0,4
        la $a0,read_x2
        syscall

        li $v0,5
        syscall
        move $t4,$v0
```

A help message is displayed (function 4) and then, the right limit is entered from the keyboard (function 5).

```
        move $t5,$t3
```

Counter ($t5) initialization with the value of the left limit.

```
again:
```

```
mul $t6,$t5,$t5
mul $t7,$t2,$t5
mul $t6,$t6,$t1
add $t6,$t6,$t7
```

Calculation of ax^2+bx.

```
beqz $t6,zero
```

If the result ($t6) is zero, then the counter value ($t5) causes this result. If $t6 is zero, then the execution flow is driven to label zero for displaying the corresponding information.

cont:

```
add $t5,$t5,1
```

Update the counter value (increase by 1)

```
ble $t5,$t4,again
```

While the right limit is not overcome, go to the label again for calculating the new function value.

```
li $v0,4
la $a0,term
syscall
```

Display a message for the program termination

```
li $v0,10
syscall
```

Program termination with the function 10

```
zero:

    li $v0,4
    la $a0,x_miden
    syscall

    li $v0,1
    move $a0,$t5
    syscall
    j cont
```

Display a help message (function 4) for the zero result and the corresponding value that causes this result.

The complete code is following.

```
#Application 8
.text 0x00400000            #Code section

start:                      #Display the message "\n a="
```

```
li $v0,4              #Load the function number
la $a0,read_a         #Load the message starting address
syscall               #Function call
```

#Read the first number
```
li $v0,5              #Load the function number
syscall               #Function call
move $t1,$v0          #Load the number in $t1
```

#Display the message "\n b="
```
li $v0,4              #Load the function number
la $a0,read_b         #Load the message starting address
syscall               #Function call
```

#Read the second number
```
li $v0,5              #Load the function number
syscall               #Function call
move $t2,$v0          #Load the number in $t2
```

#Display the message "\n[x1,x2]"
```
li $v0,4              #Load the function number
la $a0,range          #Load the message starting address
syscall               #Function call
```

#Display the message "\nx1="
```
li $v0,4              #Load the function number
la $a0,read_x1        #Load the message starting address
syscall               #Function call
```

#Read the first limit (X1)
```
li $v0,5              #Load the function number
syscall               #Function call
move $t3,$v0          #Load the number in $t3
```

#Display the message "\nx2="
```
li $v0,4              #Load the function number
la $a0,read_x2        #Load the message starting address
syscall               #Function call
```

```
                                    #Read the second limit (X2)
      li $v0,5                       #Load the function number
      syscall                        #Function call
      move $t4,$v0                   #Load the number in $t4


                              #The first limit is the initial value of the counter
      move $t5,$t3             #$t5=counter
again:
      mul $t6,$t5,$t5   #Square calculation ($t6=$t5*$t5), X^2
      mul $t7,$t2,$t5   #Product calculation ($t7=$t2*$t5), bX
      mul $t6,$t6,$t1   #Calculation $t6=$t6*$t1, AX^2
      add $t6,$t6,$t7   #Calculation $t6=$t6+$t7, AX^2+BX
      beqz $t6,zero     #If the result is zero, goto zero
cont:
      add $t5,$t5,1                   #Counter update
      ble $t5,$t4,again               #Go to again if the second limit is
                                      #not overcome


                                     #Display the message
                                     #"\nProgram termination"
      li $v0,4                        #Load the function number
      la $a0,term                     #Load the message starting address
      syscall                         #Function call


                                     #Program termination
      li $v0,10                       #Load the function number
      syscall                         #Function call


zero:                                #Display message for the value that
                                     #causes a zero result
                                     #Display the message
                                     #"\nValue for f(x)=0, x="
      li $v0,4                        #Load the function number
      la $a0,x_zero                   #Load the message starting address
      syscall                         #Function call


                                     #Display the value that causes
                                     #the zero result
      li $v0,1                        #Load the function number
      move $a0,$t5                    #Load the value to be displayed
```

```
          syscall                      #Function call
          j cont                       #Return to iteration loop for
                                       #calculating the new value

.data                                  #Data section
read_a:       .asciiz "\n a="
read_b:       .asciiz "\n b="
range:        .asciiz "\n[x1,x2]"
read_x1:      .asciiz "\nx1="
read_x2:      .asciiz "\nx2="
x_zero:       .asciiz "\nValue for f(x)=0, x="
term:         .asciiz "\nProgram termination"
```

Application 9 – Multiple iteration loops

Very often multiple iteration loops or nested loops are needed. Multiple iteration loops can be used for implementing a time delay or in general a big number of iterations. On the other hand, possible repetitions and symmetries are investigated in the logic structure of an application. Such application features can drive to smaller and optimum code and offering the opportunity to adapt the application to the real needs and specifications. In this application, a program for displaying asterisks will be developed. The asterisks have the following form:

```
*
**
***
****
*****
******
*******
```

The number of asterisks is relevant to the line that belong. In the first line, there is one asterisk, in the second line there are two asterisks, and so on. If the counter A is used, then another counter has to be used for counting the number of asterisks in the specific line. In line A, A asterisks will be displayed and the second counter will take values in the range 1 to A. Thus the general form of the iteration loops will be as follows:

For A=1 to N (where N is the number of lines that have be chosen by the user)
     For B=1 to A (where B is the numbers of asterisks per line)

The following flow chart (figure 2.10) shows the implementation logic of the iteration loops as well as the logic of the asterisks display.

Code development
```
.text 0x00400000
```

```
        li $v0,4
        la $a0,dose
        syscall


        li $v0,5
        syscall
        move $t1,$v0
```

Display the message "N=" and read a number (number of lines).

2

```
        li $t3,1
```

Initialize the line counter

```
again:
```

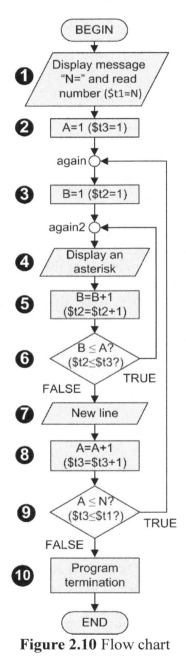

Figure 2.10 Flow chart

```
li $t2,1
```

Initialize the asterisk counter for current line

```
again2:
```

```
li $v0,4
la $a0,asteri
syscall
```

Display an asterisk

```
add $t2,$t2,1
```

Update the asterisks counter

```
ble $t2,$t3,again2
```

Go to `again2` if all the asterisks have not been displayed yet.

```
li $v0,4
la $a0,line
```

```
syscall
```

New line (change line)

```
add $t3,$t3,1
```

Update the lines counter

```
ble $t3,$t1,again
```

Go to `again` if all the lines have not been displayed yet.

```
li $v0,10
syscall
```
Program termination

```
.data
dose:       .asciiz "N="
asteri:     .asciiz "*"
line:       .asciiz "\n"
```

The complete code is following.

#Application 9	
`.text 0x00400000`	**#Code section**
	#Display the message "N="
`li $v0,4`	#Load the function number
`la $a0,dose`	#Load the message starting address
`syscall`	#Function call

```
                                    #Read   number  (number  of  lines)
     li $v0,5                       #Load the function number
     syscall                        #Function call
     move $t1,$v0                   #Load number in $t1

     li $t3,1                       #Initialize line counter
again:
     li $t2,1                       #Initialize asterisks counter
again2:
                                    #Display an asterisk
     li $v0,4                       #Load the function number
     la $a0,asteri                  #Load the message starting address
     syscall                        #Function call

     add $t2,$t2,1                  #Update asterisk counter
     ble $t2,$t3,again2             #While all the asterisks have not
                                    #been displayed, go to again2

                                    #New line
     li $v0,4                       #Load the function number
     la $a0,line                    #Load the message starting address
     syscall                        #Function call

     add $t3,$t3,1                  #Update line counter
     ble $t3,$t1,again              #While all the lines have not
                                    #been displayed, go to again

                                    #Program termination
     li $v0,10                      #Load the function number
     syscall                        #Function call

.data                               #Data section

dose:           .asciiz "N="
asteri:         .asciiz "*"
line:           .asciiz "\n"
```

Application 10 – Displaying a function in a selected range

In the programming approach of functions, iteration loops are used for producing the X values and performing the corresponding calculation. The function results are displayed arithmetically in a matrix or in a graph by combining the X and Y values. In this application, the function $f(x)=x^2$ has been chosen to be displayed. In the simulation environment there is no graphical interface and thus only the text console window will be used. A significant limitation of the console is that X and Y coordinates (columns, lines) cannot be set. Thus, the X and Y points of the function cannot be displayed. Another limitation is that only ASCII characters can be displayed on screen. Moreover, the line control can be only achieved by displaying spaces. For all the above reasons, the function will be displayed with inverted axes, due to the fact that only single symbols can be displayed in every line. The main program implements an iteration loop for the X values for a range which is given from the keyboard (X1=minimum value of X, X2=maximum value of X). For every point Y=f(x) an asterisk will be displayed. The distance of every asterisk from the horizontal inverted axis will be Y positions from the first column. Thus, for displaying an asterisk at the correct position, Y-1 spaces have to be displayed and one asterisk for every new value of Y. This practically means that one nested iteration loop must be existed for displaying Y-1 spaces before the asterisk display. The line change will be performed after the asterisk display and before the end-point of the outer iteration loop. Figure 2.11 shows the logic of the function display with the inverted axes. Note here that for Y=0 an asterisk is also displayed. If the above asterisk display (for Y=0) has to be avoided than a condition-check has to be placed for driving the execution flow directly to the next line.

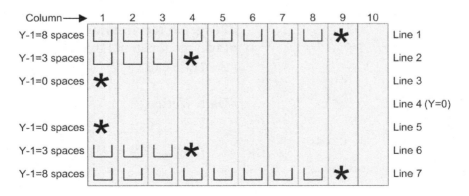

Figure 2.11 Combining spaces and asterisks [-3,3]

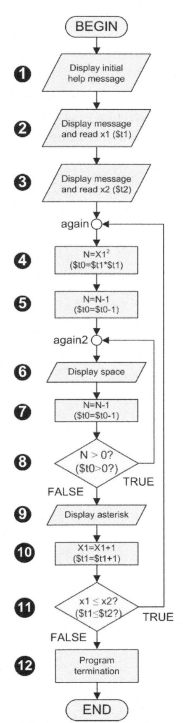

Figure 2.12 Flow chart

Figure 2.12 shows the flow chart of the application.

Code development

```
.text 0x00400000
```

```
li $v0,4
la $a0,msg
syscall
```

Display help message for the function and the value range.

```
li $v0,4
la $a0,x1
syscall

li $v0,5
syscall
move $t1,$v0
```

Display message and read the minimum value of X (X1, left limit of the range) that will be stored in $t1.

```
li $v0,4
la $a0,x2
syscall
```

```
li $v0,5
syscall
move $t2,$v0
```

Display message and read the maximum value of X (X2, right limit of the range) that will be stored in $t2. The main iteration loop will has as a minimum value the X1 (counter $t1) and as a maximum value (check value at the end of the loop) the X2.

```
again:
```

```
mul $t0,$t1,$t1
```

Calculate square ($1^2=$t1*$t1) and store in $t0

```
add  $t0,$t0,-1
```

Calculate Y-1 ($t0=$t0-1) for the spaces that will be displayed in the current line.

```
again2:
```

```
li $v0,4
la $a0,keno
syscall
```

Display a space in the current line (within the loop).

```
add $t0,$t0,-1
```

Update the space counter (after every display completion).

```
bgtz $t0,again2
```

While all the spaces have not been displayed ($t0>0) go to `again2`.

```
li $v0,4
la $a0,asteri
syscall
```

Display an asterisk (after displaying the Y-1 spaces). The message contains the character "\n" for changing the line.

```
add $t1,$t1,1
```

Update the lines counter. Every line contains spaces and one asterisk.

```
ble $t1,$t2,again
```

While X is less or equal to X2 (right limit of the range), the main iteration loop will be continued for the next value of X.

12

```
li $v0,10
syscall
```

Program termination

The complete code is following

#Application 10

`.text 0x00400000`	**#Code section**
	#Display the message "X^2, X e [x1,x2]"
`li $v0,4`	#Load the function number
`la $a0,msg`	#Load the message starting address
`syscall`	#Function call
	#Display the message "\nx1="
`li $v0,4`	#Load the function number
`la $a0,x1`	#Load the message starting address
`syscall`	#Function call
	#Read the first limit (X1)
`li $v0,5`	#Load the function number
`syscall`	#Function call
`move $t1,$v0`	#Load the number in $t1
	#Display the message "x2="
`li $v0,4`	#Load the function number
`la $a0,x2`	#Load the message starting address
`syscall`	#Function call
	#Read the second limit (X2)
`li $v0,5`	#Load the function number
`syscall`	#Function call
`move $t2,$v0`	#Load the number in $t2
`again:`	**#Main loop (outer loop)**

```
mul $t0,$t1,$t1        #Calculate Square N=X^2
add $t0,$t0,-1         #Calculate N-1 (for displaying N-1 spaces)

again2:                #Inner loop
                       #Display spaces
li $v0,4               #Load the function number
la $a0,keno            #Load the message starting address
syscall                #Function call
add $t0,$t0,-1         #Update the spaces counter
bgtz $t0,again2        #While all the spaces have not been
                       #displayed, go to again2

                       #Display an asterisk
li $v0,4               #Load the function number
la $a0,asteri          #Load the message starting address
syscall                #Function call
add $t1,$t1,1          #Update the main loop counter
ble $t1,$t2,again      #While the end of spaces has not been
                       #reached, go to again

                       #Program termination
li $v0,10              #Load the function number
syscall                #Function call

.data                  #Data section
asteri:     .asciiz "*\n"
keno:       .asciiz " "
x1:         .asciiz "\nx1="
x2:         .asciiz "x2="
msg:        .asciiz "X^2, X e [x1,x2]"
```

Figure 2.13 shows the function on the screen for the specific value range.

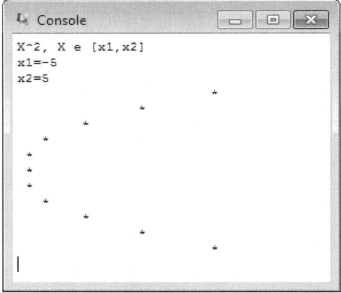

Figure 2.13 Function display on screen with inverted axes

3.3 Filling and displaying an array

Using the instructions of the previous paragraph a program for filling an array from the keyboard with 10 integer numbers can be developed. Every number is entered from the keyboard and is initially stored in a register. Thus each number is represented by 32bits or 4 bytes. This means that for 10 numbers (logic array), 40 memory locations are needed (4 locations for each number). The following code reads 10 numbers from the keyboard and the final storage is performed in the memory (array).

```
.text 0x00400000
li $t2,1                    #Loop counter
li $t1,0                    #Deviation counter

start:
                            #Read an integer from the keyboard
        li $v0,5
        syscall

        move $t0,$v0        #Load the number temporarily

                            #Store the number in array
                            #sw = store word (32 bit)
                            #Address = [arrayA]+[$t1]

        sw $t0,arrayA($t1)

        addi $t1,$t1,4      #Update deviation counter
        addi $t2,$t2,1      #Update loop counter
        ble $t2,10,start    #Condition-check of the iteration loop

        li $v0,10           #Program termination
        syscall

.data                       #Data section

                            #The array hosts
                            #data of "dimension" 2^2=4bytes
.align 2
```

```
arrayA: .space 40          #Reserve 40 bytes
                           #(10 locations x 4 bytes per location)
```

In the above code, the register $t2 is used as a single counter for ensuring that 10 numbers will be entered from the keyboard, while the register $t1 is used for calculating the deviation from the beginning of the array (arrayA). The deviation step is always 4, and is equal to the total memory locations that are needed for the storage of every number.

For displaying the array content, the instruction lw (load word) instead of sw will be used. The iteration loop is always the same (same array, 10 numbers, same deviation, etc). The next code shows the different implementation for filling and displaying the array with the 10 numbers.

(a) Filling array	(b) Displaying array

```
li $t2,1  #loop counter          li $t2,1  #loop counter
li $t1,0  #deviation counter     li $t1,0  #deviation counter

start:                           start2:

    #Read number                     #Read number
    #from keyboard                   #from array
    li $v0,5                         #lw = load word
    syscall
                                     lw $t0,arrayA($t1)
    #Temporary storage
    move $t0,$v0                     move $a0,$t0
                                     li $v0,1
    #Store number in array           syscall
    #sw = store word
                                     li $v0,4
    sw $t0,arrayA($t1)               la $a0,spacechar
                                     syscall
    #update dev. counter
    addi $t1,$t1,4                   #update dev. counter
                                     addi $t1,$t1,4
    #update loop counter
    addi $t2,$t2,1                   #update loop counter
                                     addi $t2,$t2,1
    #condition check
```

```
        ble $t2,10,start          #condition check
                                  ble $t2,10,start2
    #program termination
    li $v0,10                     #program termination
    syscall                       li $v0,10
                                  syscall
#data section
.data                         #data section
                              .data
.align 2                      spacechar: .asciiz " "
                              .align 2
arrayA: .space 40
                              arrayA: .space 40
```

3.4 Applications development

3.4.1 Basic procedures in arrays

Application 11 - Filling and displaying an array

The filling and displaying the contents of an array is based on a simple iteration loop for scanning the corresponding elements. Despite the fact that the basic difference is focused on a simple instruction (sw or lw), always the corresponding implementation is performed with two different iteration loops. This is done for offering to the user the capability to display the array contents at any time. In this application, an integer array (4 bytes per number) with 10 numbers is filled and then the corresponding contents are displayed. Moreover, during the filling procedure, a help message is displayed for informing the user which array position will be filled. For achieving this, a string has to be combined with the content of a register (i.e. "Pos[" $t2 "]=", where $t2 is the counter of the numbers that are entered from the keyboard. As shown in the flow chart of figure 3.4, the corresponding implementation includes two iteration loops.

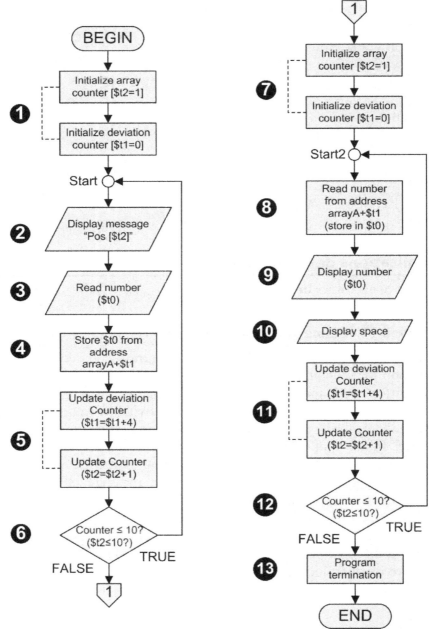

Figure 3.4 Flow chart for filling and displaying an array

Base on the above flow chart, the corresponding code is as follows:

```
.text 0x00400000
```

```
li $t2,1
```

Initialize the number counter (how many numbers will be read from the keyboard).

```
li $t1,0
```

Initialize the array deviation counter. This register will be used in combination with the address arrayA (arrayA+$t1) for accessing the array data. The above address corresponds to the first byte of the four that finally will be read.

```
start:
```

2

```
        li $v0,4
        la $a0,m1
        syscall

        li $v0,1
        move $a0,$t2
        syscall

        li $v0,4
        la $a0,m2
        syscall
```

Display a help message in the form "Pos[$t2]=" before the reading from the keyboard (where $t2 is the register for current position).

3

```
        li $v0,5
        syscall
        move $t0,$v0
```

Read the integer number from the keyboard. Store the number in $t0.

```
sw $t0,arrayA($t1)
```

Store the number (from $t0) in array (memory area) starting from the address arrayA+$t1. The rest three bytes are stored in the memory locations that follows.

```
add $t1,$t1,4
```

Update the deviation counter. The value 4 corresponds to the number of bytes to be stored in memory.

```
add $t2,$t2,1
```

Update loop counter (how many numbers will be read)

```
ble $t2,10,start
```

If all the memory locations have not been filled ($t2<=10) go to start (return to loop).

```
li $t2,1
```
Initialize the loop counter. This initialization is necessary because $t2 has already a content from the previous loop.

```
li $t1,0
```

Initialize the deviation counter in order to read the array from the beginning.

start2:

```
lw $t0,arrayA($t1)
```

Read four bytes starting from the address arrayA+$t1. The four bytes are stored in $t0.

```
li $v0,1
move $a0,$t0
syscall
```

Display the number that has just been read from the array (content of $t0)

```
li $v0,4
la $a0,spacechar
syscall
```

Display a space before read the next number

```
add $t1,$t1,4
```
Update the deviation counter

```
add $t2,$t2,1
```

Update the loop counter (how many numbers will be read)

```
ble $t2,10,start2
```

While all the numbers have not been read ($t2<=10), go to start2

```
li $v0,10
syscall
```

Program termination (function 10).

The complete code follows.

```
#Application 11
.text 0x00400000          #Code section
li $t2,1                  #Loop (number) counter
li $t1,0                  #Deviation counter

                          #Fill array

start:
                          #Display the message "Pos["
        li $v0,4          #Load the function number
        la $a0,m1         #Load the message starting address
        syscall           #Function call

                          #Display number (array location)
        li $v0,1          #Load the function number
        move $a0,$t2      #Load the number to be displayed
        syscall           #Function call

                          #Display the message "]="
        li $v0,4          #Load the function number
        la $a0,m2         #Load the message starting address
        syscall           #Function call

                          #Read number
        li $v0,5          #Load the function number
        syscall           #Function call
        move $t0,$v0      #Load the number in $t0
```

```
    sw $t0,arrayA($t1)      #Store the number
                            #starting from the
                            #address arrayA+$t1 (4 bytes)

    add $t1,$t1,4           #Update deviation counter
    add $t2,$t2,1           #Update loop counter

    ble $t2,10,start        #While all the numbers
                            #have not been read, go to start

                            #Read array
li $t2,1                    #Loop (number) counter
li $t1,0                    #Deviation counter

start2:
    lw $t0,arrayA($t1)      #Load the number starting
                            #from the address
                            #arrayA+$t1 (4 bytes)

                            #Display the number
                            #(from the array)
    li $v0,1                #Load the function number
    move $a0,$t0            #Load the number to be displayed
    syscall                 #Function call

                            #Display a space
    li $v0,4                #Load the function number
    la $a0,spacechar        #Load the message starting address
    syscall                 #Function call
    add $t1,$t1,4           #Update deviation counter
    add $t2,$t2,1           #Update loop counter

    ble $t2,10,start2       #While all the numbers have not
                            #been read, go to start2

                            #Program termination
    li $v0,10               #Load the function number
    syscall                 #Function call
```

```
.data                           #Data section
spacechar: .asciiz " "
.align 2                        #Array organization

arrayA: .space 40               #Array declaration
m1:         .asciiz "Pos["
m2:         .asciiz "]="
```

Figure 3.5 shows the application operation.

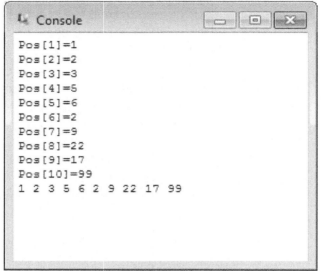

Figure 3.5 Application 11

3.4.2 Array data processing

Application 12 - Finding positive, negative and zero numbers in an array

For processing the data of any array the corresponding array elements have to be "scanned" (sequentially or randomly). Thus, iteration loops have to be implemented for the storing and reading procedures. In this application, every array element will be checked if it is positive, negative or zero. In every case an individual counter will be used. Figure 3.6 shows the corresponding flow chart.

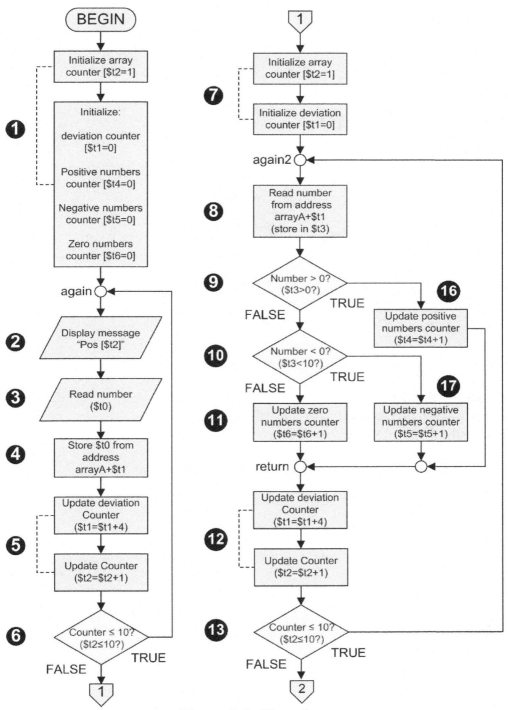

Figure 3.6a Flow chart

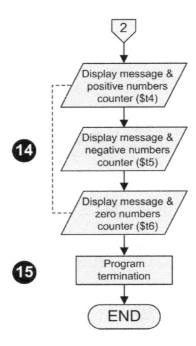

Figure 3.6b Flow chart

The algorithm of figure 3.6 can be grouped in the following sections:

(a) array fill (steps 1 to 7)
(b) array data processing (steps 8 to 16 and 21,22)
(c) results display (steps 17 to 19)

Based on the above algorithm, the code development is as follows:

```
.text 0x00400000


main:
```

1

```
    li $t2,1
```

Initialize the numbers counter (the numbers that will be stored in the array). Despite the fact that the other registers are not initialized, the corresponding content is zero within the simulator environment. In a real microprocessor the initialization of the registers is necessary.

```
again:
```

```
    li $v0,4
    la $a0,mes1
    syscall


    li $v0,1
    move $a0,$t2
    syscall


    li $v0,4
    la $a0,mes2
    syscall
```

Display a help message for the current array location which is under filling. Due to the fact that the message consists of different parts (alphanumeric, integer) different functions will be used.

```
    li $v0,5
    syscall
    move $t0,$v0
```

Read an integer number from the keyboard for the current array location

```
    sw $t0,arrayA($t1)
```

Store the number in array starting from the address arrayA+$t1. Note that for every number, 4 bytes are finally used in the corresponding register. If for example the number 1 is entered, then inside the register, the value 00000001 will be stored (4 bytes in total).

```
add $t1,$t1,4
```

Update the deviation counter. After the counter increment, the next number will be stored from the address arrayA + $t1.

```
add $t2,$t2,1
```

Update loop counter (for reading 10 numbers)

```
ble $t2,10,again
```

If all the numbers have not been read ($t2<=10), then go to again

```
li $t2,1
```

Initialize the loop counter (how many numbers will be read from array)

```
li $t1,0
```

Initialize the deviation counter

```
again2:
```

```
    lw $t3,arrayA($t1)
```

Read a number (4 bytes) starting from the address arrayA+$t1 (store the number in $t3)

```
    bgtz $t3,einai_meg_msg
```

If the number ($t3) is greater than zero (positive), then go to einai_meg_msg for updating the corresponding counter

```
    bltz $t3,einai_mik_msg
```

If the number ($t3) is less than zero (negative), then go to einai_mik_msg for updating the corresponding counter. For reaching that point from the execution flow, the previous condition-check (bgtz) is false.

```
    add $t6,$t6,1
```

Update the zero numbers counter (the previous condition-checks are FALSE).

```
return:
```

```
    add $t1,$t1,4
```

Update deviation counter

```
add $t2,$t2,1
```

Update loop counter (numbers to be read from array)

```
ble $t2,10,again2
```

If all the numbers have not been read ($t2<=10), go to `again2`

```
li $v0,4
la $a0,meg_msg
syscall

li $v0,1
move $a0,$t4
syscall
```

Display a help message and the content of the positive numbers counter

```
li $v0,4
la $a0,mik_msg
syscall

li $v0,1
move $a0,$t5
syscall
```

Display a help message and the content of the negative numbers counter

```
li $v0,4
la $a0,miden_msg
syscall

li $v0,1
move $a0,$t6
syscall
```

Display a help message and the content of the zero numbers counter

```
li $v0,10
syscall
```

Program termination (function 10)

```
einai_meg_msg:
    add $t4,$t4,1
    j return
```

Update positive numbers counter and return to loop

```
einai_mik_msg:
    add $t5,$t5,1
    j return
```

Update negative numbers counter and return to loop

The complete code is following.

#Application 12

```
.text 0x00400000        #Code section
main:

    li $t2,1            #Loop counter
                        #$t1=deviation counter
                        #$t4=positive numbers counter
                        #$t5=negative numbers counter
                        #$t6=zero numbers counter


again:                  #Fill array

                        #Display the message "Pos["
    li $v0,4            #Load the function number
    la $a0,mes1         #Load the message starting address
    syscall             #Function call

                        #Display counter (current number)
    li $v0,1            #Load the function number
    move $a0,$t2        #Load the number to be displayed
    syscall             #Function call

                        #Display the message "]="
    li $v0,4            #Load the function number
    la $a0,mes2         #Load the message starting address
    syscall             #Function call

                        #Read number (keyboard)
    li $v0,5            #Load the function number
    syscall             #Function call
    move $t0,$v0        #Load number in $t0

    sw $t0,arrayA($t1)  #Store number starting from
                        #the address arrayA+$t1 (4 byte)

    add $t1,$t1,4       #Update deviation counter
    add $t2,$t2,1       #Update loop counter

    ble $t2,10,again    #If all the number have not
                        #been read go to again
```

```
                              #Read array
      li $t2,1                #Initialize loop counter
      li $t1,0                #Initialize deviation counter

again2:
      lw $t3,arrayA($t1)      #Read number starting from
                              #arrayA+$t1


      bgtz $t3,einai_meg_msg      #If number > 0
      bltz $t3,einai_mik_msg      #If number < 0
      add $t6,$t6,1               #Update zero numbers counter

return:                       #return point

      add $t1,$t1,4           #Update deviation counter
      add $t2,$t2,1           #Update loop counter

      ble $t2,10,again2       #If all the numbers have
                              #not been read, go to again2

                              #Display the message "\n(>0):"
      li $v0,4                #Load the function number
      la $a0,meg_msg          #Load the message starting address
      syscall                 #Function call

                              #Display positive numbers counter
      li $v0,1                #Load the function number
      move $a0,$t4            #Load the number to be displayed
      syscall                 #Function call

                              #Display the message "\n(<0):"
      li $v0,4                #Load the function number
      la $a0,mik_msg          #Load the message starting address
      syscall                 #Function call

                              #Display negative numbers counter
      li $v0,1                #Load the number to be displayed
      move $a0,$t5            #Load the message starting address
```

```
        syscall                    #Function call

                                   #Display the message "\n(=0):"
        li $v0,4                   #Load the function number
        la $a0,miden_msg           #Load the message starting address
        syscall                    #Function call

                                   #Display zero numbers counter
        li $v0,1                   #Load the function number
        move $a0,$t6               #Load the number to be displayed
        syscall                    #Function call

                                   #Program termination
        li $v0,10                  #Load the function number
        syscall                    #Function call

einai_meg_msg:                     #Section for positive numbers
        add $t4,$t4,1              #Update positive numbers counter
        j return                   #Return to main loop

einai_mik_msg:                     #Section for negative numbers
        add $t5,$t5,1              #Update negative numbers counter
        j return                   #Return to main loop

.data                              #Data section
mes1: .asciiz "Pos["
mes2: .asciiz "]="
meg_msg: .asciiz "\n(>0):"
mik_msg: .asciiz "\n(<0):"
miden_msg: .asciiz "\n(=0):"

.align 2                           #Array organization
arrayA: .space 40                  #Array declaration
```

Figure 3.7 shows the application execution.

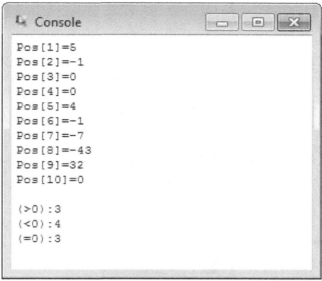

Figure 3.7 Application 12

Application 13 - Finding the maximum number in an array

The finding of the maximum or minimum number in an array constitutes a classic application. Assume an array of 10 numbers. Initially it is assumed that the maximum number exists in the first location of the array. This number (maximum) is compared with the number of the next location in the array. For simplicity reasons the above comparison can be performed from the first location. If the number of the current array location is greater than the maximum number, then a new maximum number has been found. Every time a greater number is found, then this number is compared with the next one. Figure 3.8 shows the algorithm logic.

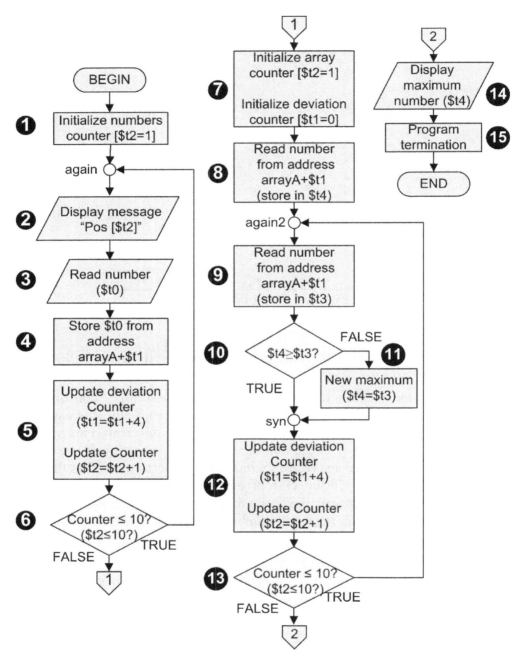

Figure 3.8 Finding the maximum number

Based on the above flow chart, the code development is as follows:

```
.text 0x00400/000
```

```
        li $t2,1
```

Initialize the loop counter (how many numbers will be read)

```
again:
```

```
        li $v0,4
        la $a0,mes1
        syscall

        move $a0,$t2
        li $v0,1
        syscall


        li $v0,4
        la $a0,mes2
        syscall
```

Display a help message before entering the number from the keyboard.

```
        li $v0,5
        syscall
        move $t0,$v0
```

Read a number from the keyboard (store the number in $t0)

```
sw $t0,arrayA($t1)
```

Store the number in the array starting from the address arrayA+$t1.

```
add $t1,$t1,4
```

Update deviation counter

```
add $t2,$t2,1
```

Update loop counter

```
ble $t2,10,again
```

While all the numbers have not been stored, go to again (return to loop)

```
li $t2,1
```

Initialize loop counter

```
li $t1,0
```

Initialize deviation counter ($t4 contains an out of bounds value from the previous loop)

```
lw $t4,arrayA($t1)
```

Read the first location of the array (store in $t4, assuming that the maximum number is contained in the first location)

```
again2:
```

```
lw $t3,arrayA($t1)
```

Read the next number (start reading again from the first array location for simplicity reasons, does not affect the result)

```
bgt $t4,$t3,syn
```

If the current maximum value ($t4) is still greater than the value of the current array location ($t3), then the maximum number does not change and the execution flow continues from the label syn

```
move $t4,$t3
```

If the current maximum number ($t4) is not greater than the current array number, then a new maximum number has been found and the register $t4 is updated. Note that a new maximum is also assumed if the current maximum number is equal to current array number (for simplicity reasons).

`syn:`

```
    add $t1,$t1,4
```

Update deviation counter

```
    add $t2,$t2,1
```
Update loop counter

```
    ble $t2,10,again2
```

If all the numbers have not been read, go to `again2`

```
    li $v0,4
    la $a0,max_msg
    syscall

    li $v0,1
    move $a0,$t4
    syscall
```

Display a help message and the maximum number that has been found in the array

```
li $v0,10
syscall
```

Program termination (function 10)

The complete code is following.

#Application 13

```
.text 0x00400000        #Code section
    li $t2,1            #Initialize loop counter
again:
                        #Display the message "Pos["
    li $v0,4            #Load the function number
    la $a0,mes1         #Load the message starting address
    syscall             #Function call

    move $a0,$t2        #Display current array location
    li $v0,1            #Load the function number
    syscall             #Function call

                        #Display the message "]="
    li $v0,4            #Load the function number
    la $a0,mes2         #Load the message starting address
    syscall             #Function call

                        #Read number (keyboard)
    li $v0,5            #Load the function number
    syscall             #Function call
    move $t0,$v0        #Load the number in $t0



    sw $t0,arrayA($t1)  #Store the number starting from
                        #the address arrayA+$t1 (4 bytes)

    add $t1,$t1,4       #Update deviation counter
    add $t2,$t2,1       #Update loop counter
    ble $t2,10,again    #If all the numbers have not been
```

```
                                #read, go to again

        li $t4,0                #Assume that the maximum number exists in
                                #the first array location
        li $t2,1                #Initialize loop counter
        li $t1,0                #Initialize deviation counter
        lw $t4,arrayA($t1)      #Read number (starting from the
                                #address arrayA+$t1)
again2:
        lw $t3,arrayA($t1)      #Read number (starting from the
                                #address arrayA+$t1)

        bgt $t4,$t3,syn         #If the current number is less or equal
                                #to maximum, then the next array
                                #number is processing

        move $t4,$t3            #If a new maximum is found,
                                #then update $t4
syn:

        add $t1,$t1,4           #Update deviation counter
        add $t2,$t2,1           #Update loop counter
        ble $t2,10,again2       #If all the numbers have
                                #not been read, go to again2

                                #Display the message "\nmax="
        li $v0,4                #Load the function number
        la $a0,max_msg          #Load the message starting address
        syscall                 #Function call

                                #Display the maximum
        li $v0,1                #Load the function number
        move $a0,$t4            #Load the number to be displayed
        syscall                 #Function call

        li $v0,10               #Program termination
        syscall                 #Function call

.data                           #Data section
mes1: .asciiz "Pos["
mes2: .asciiz "]="
max_msg: .asciiz "\nmax="
```

```
.align 2                    #Array organization
arrayA: .space 40           #Array declaration
```

Figure 3.9 shows the application execution (finding the maximum number in an array).

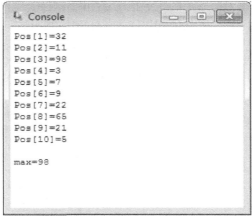

Figure 3.9 Application execution

Application 14 - Counting symbols in a character array

In this application, a string (alphanumeric) is entered from the keyboard and the corresponding occurrence frequency of every character is counted. For achieving that, a separate counter for every symbol (character) is used. After symbol counting completion the corresponding occurrence frequency is displayed as an asterisks histogram. The program supports the input of seven symbols. Moreover it is assumed that the symbols belong to the set {a,b,c,d,e,f,g}. The ASCII code for every symbol in the set is shown in table 3.2.

| Table 3.2 Symbols ASCII code ||
Symbol	ASCII
a	97
b	98
c	99
d	100
e	101
f	102
g	103

As mentioned before, a separate counter will be used for every symbol. That means that seven counters will be used in total. Additionally, the asterisks histogram will be based on the above symbol counters. The worst programing technique is to use registers as symbols counters. Thus, the above counters will be implemented in the same array where every location will corresponds to a symbol counter. For updating a counter, a deviation counter will be used. For implementing an optimized array access, the deviation counter will be derived directly from the corresponding symbol. Due to the fact that every symbol has a unique ASCII code, the corresponding deviation counter can be derived by subtracting the number 97.

Figure 3.10 shows the logic for converting an ASCII code to a deviation counter in order to update the corresponding symbol counter.

Symbol	ASCII			Counter array	
a	97	97-97= $\boxed{0}$	Stats+ $\boxed{0}$		Counter for symbol 'a'
b	98	98-97= $\boxed{1}$	Stats+ $\boxed{1}$		Counter for symbol 'b'
c	99	99-97= $\boxed{2}$	Stats+ $\boxed{2}$		Counter for symbol 'c'
d	100	100-97= $\boxed{3}$	Stats+ $\boxed{3}$		Counter for symbol 'd'
e	101	101-97= $\boxed{4}$	Stats+ $\boxed{4}$		Counter for symbol 'e'
f	102	102-97= $\boxed{5}$	Stats+ $\boxed{5}$		Counter for symbol 'f'
g	103	103-97= $\boxed{6}$	Stats+ $\boxed{6}$		Counter for symbol 'g'

Figure 3.10 Convert ASCII code to array deviation

If for example the symbol 'a' has been read, then the subtraction 'a'-97 (97-97) will give a zero result. Thus the content of the counter stats+0 will be increased. This approach is based on the fact that only one byte is used for every symbol counter (one memory location for every counter). Moreover, every symbol is one byte and thus, only one memory location is needed. Note that the instructions lb and sb (b=byte) are used in the program.

Figure 3.11 shows the flow chart of the application. Based on the corresponding algorithm, two procedures are implemented:

(a) String input and occurrence frequency counting (steps 1 to 9)

(b) Read array and display frequency histogram (steps 10 to 19)

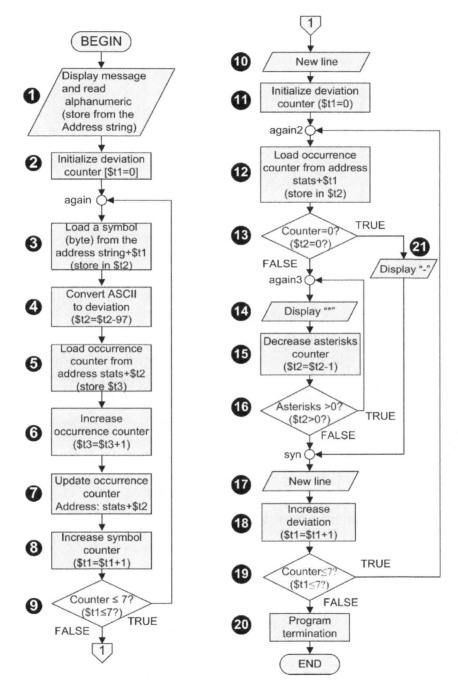

Figure 3.11 Flow chart

Code development

```
.text 0x00400000
```

```
li $v0,4
la $a0,read_string
syscall


li $v0,8
la $a0,string


li $a1,8
syscall
```

The string is entered using the function 8. The function number is always loaded in $v0, while two more registers are needed. The $a0 has to point to the starting address where the string will be stored, while $a1 hosts the string length. For using the function 8 correctly, the corresponding memory area has to be declared. The starting address will be declared through a label.

```
li $t1,0
```

Initialize deviation counter for reading the string

```
again:
```

```
lb $t2,string($t1)
```

Load one byte (one symbol) from the memory area where the string is stored. This byte will be loaded from the address string+$t1. Note that one memory address is used due to the fact than only one byte is needed.

```
sub $t2,$t2,97
```

Subtract from ASCII (of the symbol) the number 97 in order to use the corresponding deviation within the occurrence frequency array

```
lb $t3,stats($t2)
```

For updating the corresponding symbol counter, one byte has to be read from the array in order to increase by 1. Thus the counter of the address stats+$t2 is loaded in $t3

```
add $t3,$t3,1
```

Update counter (increase by 1)

```
sb $t3,stats($t2)
```

After the counter update (is stored temporarily in $t3), the result is stored in the same address (stats+$t2). Note that the same deviation is used as previously

```
add $t1,$t1,1
```

Before the end of the first loop (read the string and update the corresponding counters), the symbols counter (how many symbols will be read from the keyboard) is updated

```
ble $t1,7,again
```

If all the symbols have not been read, then the execution flow returns to loop (the check value is the number of symbols in the string)

```
li $v0,4
la $a0,line
syscall
```

Change line before display the histogram

```
li $t1,0
```

Initialize the deviation counter for accessing the occurrence frequency array

```
again2:
```

```
lb $t2,stats($t1)
```

Read the counter value from address stats+$t1.

```
beqz $t2,stats0
```

If the counter value is zero (the corresponding symbol does not exist in the string), then only the symbol '-' is displayed

```
again3:
```

```
li $v0,4
la $a0,star
syscall
```

Display an asterisk. The number of asterisks is based on the corresponding occurrence frequency counter. At step 12 the counter value is loaded in $t2 which is used as a counter in the asterisks loop. Thus, the number of asterisks is proportional to the counter content.

```
add $t2,$t2,-1
```

Update loop counter (for the asterisks)

```
bgtz $t2,again3
```

If all the asterisks have not been displayed, return to loop

```
syn:
```

```
li $v0,4
la $a0,line
syscall
```

The new line is inserted when all the asterisks for the current symbol have been displayed

```
add $t1,$t1,1
```

Update counter for reading from the occurrence frequency array

```
ble $t1,7,again2
```

If all the occurrence frequency array has not been read, return to loop

```
        li $v0,10
        syscall
```
Program termination with function 10

```
stats0:
        li $v0,4
        la $a0,tip
        syscall
        j syn
```

Display the symbol '-' if the content of the corresponding counter is zero. The complete code is following.

#Application 14

```
.text 0x00400000              #Code section

                              #Display the message "String:"
        li $v0,4              #Load the function number
        la $a0,read_string    #Load the message starting address
        syscall               #Function call

                              #Read string (keyboard)
        li $v0,8              #Load the function number
        la $a0,string         #Load the starting address
                              #for storing the string
```

```
        li $a1,8              #Set string length
        syscall              #Function call

        li $t1,0             #Counter for reading
                             #the string from memory
again:

        lb $t2,string($t1)   #Load symbol (byte)
                             #from address string+$t1
        sub $t2,$t2,97       #Convert ASCII to deviation
        lb $t3,stats($t2)    #Load current occurrence
                             #frequency counter
        add $t3,$t3,1        #Update counter
        sb $t3,stats($t2)    #Store counter in the same address
        add $t1,$t1,1        #Update loop counter
        ble $t1,7,again      #While the whole string has not been
                             #read, go to again
```

#Display statistics (histogram)
```
                             #New line
        li $v0,4             #Load the function number
        la $a0,line          #Load the message starting address
        syscall              #function call

        li $t1,0             #Counter for occurrence
                             #frequency array
again2:
        lb $t2,stats($t1)    #Load counter in stats+$t1
        beqz $t2,stats0      #If the counter is zero, go to
                             #stats0 (display "-")

        again3:
                             #Display asterisks if the
                             #counter is not zero
            li $v0,4         #Load the function number
            la $a0,star      #Load the message starting address
            syscall          #Function call
            add $t2,$t2,-1   #Update asterisks counter
        bgtz $t2,again3      #While the counter in not zero,
                             #go to again3
syn:
```

```
                                  #New line
      li $v0,4                    #Load the function number
      la $a0,line                #Load the message starting address
      syscall                    #Function call

add $t1,$t1,1                    #Update counter
ble $t1,7,again2                 #While the array end is not reached

                                  #Program termination
      li $v0,10                  #Load the function number
      syscall                    #Function call

                                  #Display "-" for a non-existing
                                  #symbol in the string
stats0:
      li $v0,4                   #Load the function number
      la $a0,tip                 #Load the message starting address
      syscall                    #Function call
      j syn                      #Return to main loop

.data                            #Data section

read_string:    .asciiz "String:"
star:           .asciiz "*"
string:         .space 8    #Reserve string area
stats:          .space 8    #Occurrence frequency array
line:           .asciiz "\n"
msg:            .asciiz "\nstats="
tip:            .asciiz "\n-"
```

Figure 3.12 shows the histogram based on the symbol occurrence frequency.

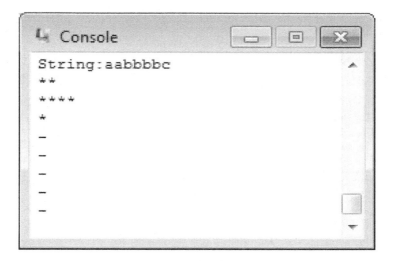

Figure 3.12 Application execution

3.4.3 Operations with arrays

Application 15 - Swapping data between arrays

In this application, the content of two one dimensional arrays will be exchanged (swap). The swapping operation will be performed for each array location. The swapping operation for two arrays A and B will be performed as follows:

temp=A[i]
A[i]=B[i]
B[i]=temp

Initially, the element i of the array A (i.e. A[i]) is stored temporarily in a variable temp. Next, the element B[i] is stored in the location i of the array A (i.e. A[i]) and finally, the B[i] is update from the content of the temporary variable temp which initially hosts the A[i]. Thus, the swapping between elements A[i] and B[i] is achieved. In the corresponding program that will be developed, the arrays A and B are initially filled. After that, the swapping operation will be performed and finally the corresponding array contents will be displayed. Figure 3.13 shows the corresponding flow chart.

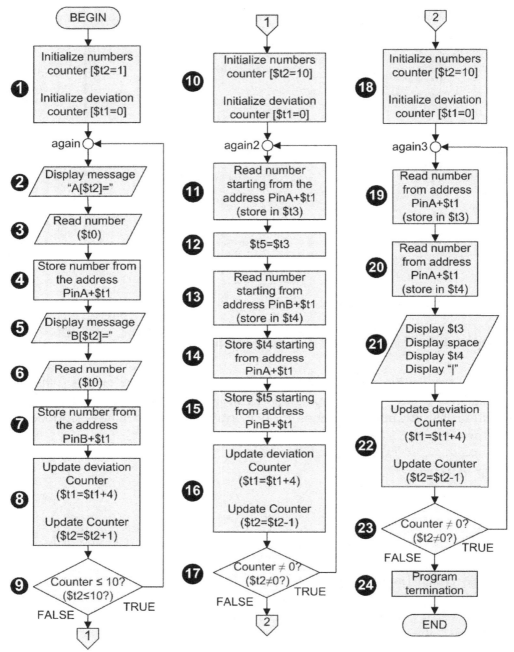

Figure 3.13 Flow chart

Code development

```
.text 0x00400000
```

```
li $t2,1
```

Initialize the numbers counter (numbers to be read and stored in array). In this application, each array will host 10 numbers in total. For avoiding an additional iteration loop, the two arrays will be filled in the same loop.

```
li $t1,0
```

Initialize the deviation counter for storing each number in the correct array location

```
again:
```

❷

```
li $v0,4
la $a0,mesA
syscall


li $v0,1
move $a0,$t2
syscall


li $v0,4
la $a0,mesC
syscall
```

Display the message in the form "A[$t2]=", where $t2 shows the current array location. The above message combines an alphanumeric and a numerical part

```
li $v0,5
syscall
move $t0,$v0
```
Read a number (keyboard) for the first array

```
sw $t0,pinA($t1)
```

Store the first number in the array starting from the address pinA+$t1

```
li $v0,4
la $a0,mesB
syscall
```

```
li $v0,1
move $a0,$t2
syscall
```

```
li $v0,4
la $a0,mesC
syscall
```

Display the message in the form "B[$t2]=", where $t2 represents the current array location

```
li $v0,5
syscall
move $t0,$v0
```

Read a number (keyboard) for the second array

```
sw $t0,pinB($t1)
```

Store the second number in the array starting from the address pinB+$t1

```
addi $t1,$t1,4
```

Update deviation counter (common counter for both arrays)

```
add $t2,$t2,1
```

Update the main counter (how many number will be read from the keyboard)

```
ble $t2,10,again
```

If all the numbers have not been read, continue from the starting point of the loop

```
li $t2,10
```

Initialize numbers counter

```
li $t1,0
```

Initialize deviation counter for accessing the arrays A and B

```
again2:
```

```
    lw $t3,pinA($t1)
```

Load in $t3 the stored number from the first array starting from the pinA+$t1 (i.e. $t3=A[i]).

```
    move $t5,$t3
```

Store the number temporarily in $t5 ($t5=$t3). Based on the above instruction, the register $t3 contains the number that has been read from the array

```
    lw $t4,pinB($t1)
```

Load in $t4 the stored number from the second array starting from the address pinB+$t1 (i.e. $t4=B[i])

```
    sw $t4,pinA($t1)
```

Store in the first array (A[]) the number that has been read from the corresponding location of the second array (B[])

```
    sw $t5,pinB($t1)
```

Store the content of the first array (A[] which is temporarily stored in $t5) in the corresponding location of the second array. After this instruction the swapping procedure has been completed for the current array location.

```
addi $t1,$t1,4
```

Update deviation counter (for the first and second array)

```
sub $t2,$t2,1
```

Update the numbers counter (numbers to be read from every array)

```
bnez $t2,again2
```

If all the numbers have not been read, then the execution flow is continued from again2. In this implementation, the loop counter starts from 10 to 1, but this does not change anything in the corresponding logic.

```
li $t2,10
```

Initialize the numbers counter for displaying the arrays content in order to verify the swapping operation.

```
li $t1,0
```

Initialize deviation counter for accessing the two arrays

```
again3:
```

```
lw $t3,pinA($t1)
```

Load the number from the first array (A[]) and store in $t3.

20

```
lw $t4,pinB($t1)
```

Load the number from the second array (B[]) and store in $t4.

21

```
li $v0,1
move $a0,$t3
syscall

li $v0,4
la $a0,spacechar
syscall

li $v0,1
move $a0,$t4
syscall

li $v0,4
la $a0,bar
syscall
```

Display the two numbers (A[i] and B[i]) with one space between them. The display operation is completed with a vertical line. With this method the number pairs are separated on the screen between the two arrays.

```
addi $t1,$t1,4
```

Update deviation counter

```
sub $t2,$t2,1
```

Update numbers counter

```
bnez $t2,again3
```

If all the numbers have not been read, the operation is continued.

```
li $v0,10
syscall
```

Program termination with the function 10

The complete code is following.

```
#Application 15
.text 0x00400000              #Code section

        li $t2,1              #Numbers counter
        li $t1,0             #Deviation counter
again:
                             #Display the message "A["
        li $v0,4             #Load the function number
        la $a0,mesA          #Load the message starting address
        syscall              #Function call

                             #Display current array location
        li $v0,1             #Load the function number
        move $a0,$t2         #load the number to be displayed
        syscall              #Function call
```

```
                              #Display the message "]="
li $v0,4                      #Load the function number
la $a0,mesC                   #Load the message starting address
syscall                       #Function call

                              #Read number (keyboard)
li $v0,5                      #Load the function number
syscall                       #Function call

move $t0,$v0                  #Load the number in $v0

sw $t0,pinA($t1)              #Store the number in the first array
                              #starting from the address pinA+$t1

                              #Display the message "B["
li $v0,4                      #Load the function number
la $a0,mesB                   #Load the message starting address
syscall                       #Function call

                              #Display current array location
li $v0,1                      #Load the function number
move $a0,$t2                  #Load the number to be displayed
syscall                       #Function call

                              #Display the message "]="
li $v0,4                      #Load the function number
la $a0,mesC                   #Load the message starting address
syscall                       #Function call

                              #Read number (keyboard)
li $v0,5                      #Load the function number
syscall                       #Function call

move $t0,$v0                  #Load the number in $v0

sw $t0,pinB($t1)              #Store the number in the second array
                              #starting from the address pinB+$t1

addi $t1,$t1,4                #Update deviation counter
```

```
        add $t2,$t2,1              #Update loop counter

        ble $t2,10,again          #While all the numbers have not been
                                   #read, go to again

        li $t2,10                  #Initialize numbers counter
        li $t1,0                   #Initialize deviation counter

again2:
        lw $t3,pinA($t1)           #Load the number from the first array
                                   #starting from the address pinA+$t1

        move $t5,$t3               #Load the number in $t5
        lw $t4,pinB($t1)           #Load the number from the
                                   #second array starting from
                                   #the address pinB+$t1

        sw $t4,pinA($t1)           #Store the second number
        sw $t5,pinB($t1)           #Store the first number
        addi $t1,$t1,4             #Update deviation counter

        sub $t2,$t2,1              #Update numbers counter
        bnez $t2,again2            #While the counter is not zero,
                                   #go to again2

                                   #Display the new arrays content

        li $t2,10                  #Numbers counter
        li $t1,0                   #Deviation counter

again3:
        lw $t3,pinA($t1)           #Read from the first array

        lw $t4,pinB($t1)           #Read from the second array

                                   #Display the content of the first array
        li $v0,1                   #Load the function number
        move $a0,$t3               #Load the number to be displayed
        syscall                    #Function call
```

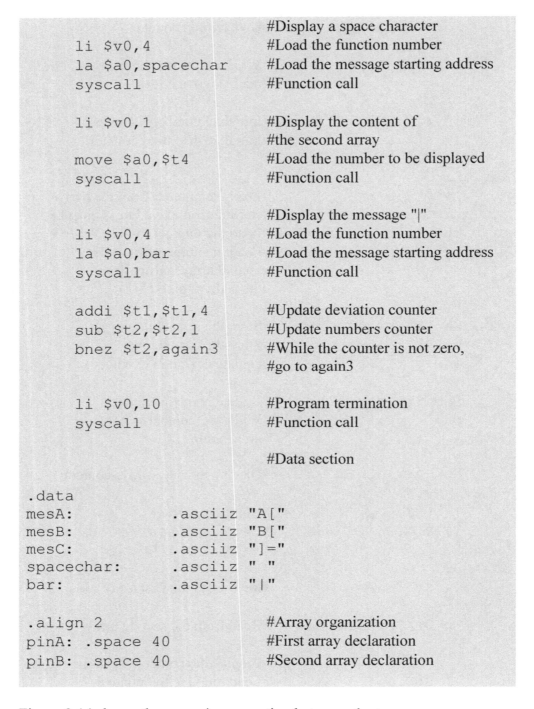

```
                                    #Display a space character
        li $v0,4                    #Load the function number
        la $a0,spacechar            #Load the message starting address
        syscall                     #Function call

        li $v0,1                    #Display the content of
                                    #the second array
        move $a0,$t4                #Load the number to be displayed
        syscall                     #Function call

                                    #Display the message "|"
        li $v0,4                    #Load the function number
        la $a0,bar                  #Load the message starting address
        syscall                     #Function call

        addi $t1,$t1,4              #Update deviation counter
        sub $t2,$t2,1               #Update numbers counter
        bnez $t2,again3             #While the counter is not zero,
                                    #go to again3

        li $v0,10                   #Program termination
        syscall                     #Function call

                                    #Data section

.data
mesA:              .asciiz "A["
mesB:              .asciiz "B["
mesC:              .asciiz "]="
spacechar:         .asciiz " "
bar:               .asciiz "|"

.align 2                            #Array organization
pinA: .space 40                     #First array declaration
pinB: .space 40                     #Second array declaration
```

Figure 3.14 shows the swapping operation between the two arrays.

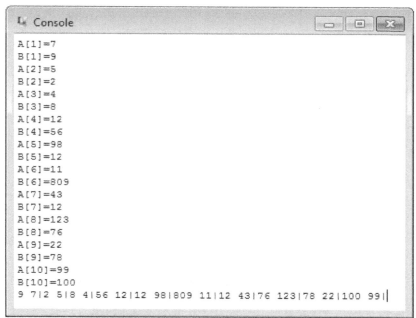

Figure 3.14 Application execution

Application 16 – Multiplying a number with an array

As shown in previous applications, the two basic array operations are, (a) array "scanning" (filling and reading) and (b) accessing array locations for data processing. In this application, the same iteration loops as previously will be used. The only difference is the operation of multiplication. More precisely, every array element will be multiplied with an integer number and the corresponding result will be stored at the same array location. For optimizing the program code, the display operation will be implemented in the same loop for the multiplication. Figure 3.15 shows the operation of multiplication of an integer number with an array.

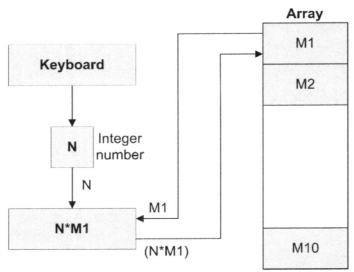

Figure 3.15 Multiplying an integer number with an array

As shows in figure 3.15, the number N that is entered from the keyboard is multiplied with the corresponding array element (in the example with M1) and the result is stored in the same array location. This operation is repeated for every array element. Based on the above method, the final results are stored in the same array. Figure 3.16 shows the corresponding flow chart.

Code development

```
.text 0x00400000
```

```
        li $v0,4
        la $a0,read_n
        syscall


        li $v0,5
        syscall
        move $t4,$v0
```

Initially, an integer number is read from the keyboard. This number will be multiplied with every element of the array. A help message is also displayed before reading the integer number.

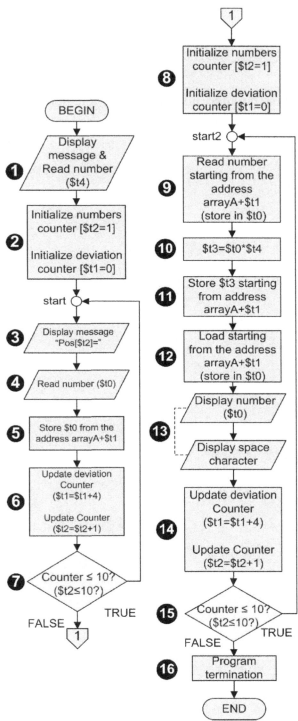

Figure 3.16 Flow chart

```
li $t2,1
```

Initialize the numbers counter (number of array elements)

```
li $t1,0
```

Initialize deviation counter

```
start:
```

```
    li $v0,4
    la $a0,m1
    syscall

    li $v0,1
    move $a0,$t2
    syscall

    li $v0,4
    la $a0,m2
    syscall
```

Before the read of every number, a help message in the form "Pos[$t2]=" is displayed ($t2 is the counter)

```
    li $v0,5
    syscall
```

```
move $t0,$v0
```

Read an integer number for the current array location

```
sw $t0,arrayA($t1)
```

Store the number in array starting from the address arrayA+$t1.

```
add $t1,$t1,4
```

Update deviation counter

```
add $t2,$t2,1
```

Update numbers counter

```
ble $t2,10,start
```

If all the array locations have not been filled, go to start

```
li $t2,1
```

Initialize the numbers counter for reading the array

```
li $t1,0
```

Initialize deviation counter

```
start2:
```

```
    lw $t0,arrayA($t1)
```

Read the current array location (starting from the address arrayA+$t1).

```
    mul $t3,$t0,$t4
```

Multiply the current array location ($t0) with the integer number ($t4). The operation $t3=$t0*$t4 will be performed

```
    sw $t3,arrayA($t1)
```

The product (the multiplication result in $t3) will be stored in the current array location starting from the address arrayA+$t1

```
    lw $t0,arrayA($t1)
```

For verifying the above operation, every array location will be read and displayed.

```
li $v0,1
move $a0,$t0
syscall


li $v0,4
la $a0,spacechar
syscall
```

Display number (current array location)

```
add $t1,$t1,4
```

Update deviation counter

```
add $t2,$t2,1
```

Update numbers counter

```
ble $t2,10,start2
```

If all the array elements have not been read, go to start2

```
li $v0,10
syscall
```

Program termination with function 10

The complete code is following.

#Application 16

```
.text 0x00400000        #Code section
                        #Display the message "N="
li $v0,4                #Load the function number
la $a0,read_n           #Load the message starting address
syscall                 #Function call

                        #Read number for multiplication
li $v0,5                #Load the function number
syscall                 #Function call
move $t4,$v0            #Load the number in $t4
                        #Fill array
li $t2,1                #Numbers counter
li $t1,0                #Deviation counter

start:
                        #Display the message "Pos["
    li $v0,4            #Load the function number
    la $a0,m1           #Load the message starting address
    syscall            #Function call

                        #Display current array location
    li $v0,1            #Load the function number
    move $a0,$t2       #Load the number to be displayed
    syscall            #Function call

                        #Display the message "]="
    li $v0,4            #Load the function number
    la $a0,m2           #Load the message starting address
    syscall            #Function call

                        #Read number for array
    li $v0,5            #Load the function number
    syscall            #Function call
    move $t0,$v0       #Load the number in $t0

    sw $t0,arrayA($t1)  #Store the number starting
```

```
                               #from the address arrayA+$t1

    add $t1,$t1,4              #Update deviation counter
    add $t2,$t2,1              #Update numbers counter
    ble $t2,10,start           #While all the numbers have
                               #not been read, go to start

li $t2,1                       #Numbers counter
li $t1,0                       #Deviation counter

start2:
    lw $t0,arrayA($t1)         #Read number from array
    mul $t3,$t0,$t4            #Multiply array elements
                               #with number
    sw $t3,arrayA($t1)         #Store the result
                               #in the same array location
    lw $t0,arrayA($t1)         #Read again from array


                               #Display results from array
    li $v0,1                   #Load the function number
    move $a0,$t0               #Load the number to be displayed
    syscall                    #Function call

                               #Display a space character
    li $v0,4                   #Load the function number
    la $a0,spacechar           #Load the message starting address
    syscall                    #Function call

    add $t1,$t1,4              #Update deviation counter
    add $t2,$t2,1              #Update numbers counter
    ble $t2,10,start2          #While all the numbers have
                               #not been read, go to start2

    li $v0,10                  #Program termination
    syscall                    #Function call
.data                          #Data section
spacechar: .asciiz " "
.align 2
arrayA:    .space 40
m1:        .asciiz "Pos["
```

```
m2:         .asciiz "]="
read_n:     .asciiz "N="
```

Figure 3.17 shows the result from the multiplication of the integer number with an array. In the example of figure 3.17, the array elements are multiplied with the number 3.

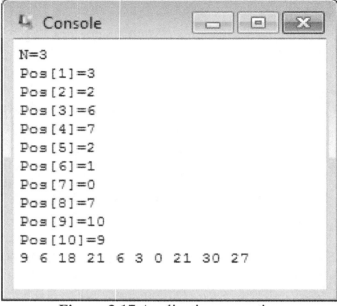

Figure 3.17 Application execution

3.4.4 Subprograms and menus for arrays management

Application 17 – Array management through a selection menu

Until now the array filling and processing have been presented. When the user wants to select which array operation to activate, the corresponding program has to offer a selection menu. An example menu is shown in figure 3.18.

```
***********************
* 1. Fill array
* 2. Display array
* 3. Selection C
* 0. Exit
***********************
SELECTION (1-3 or 0):"
```

Figure 3.18 Selection menu

The flow chart is shown in figure 3.19

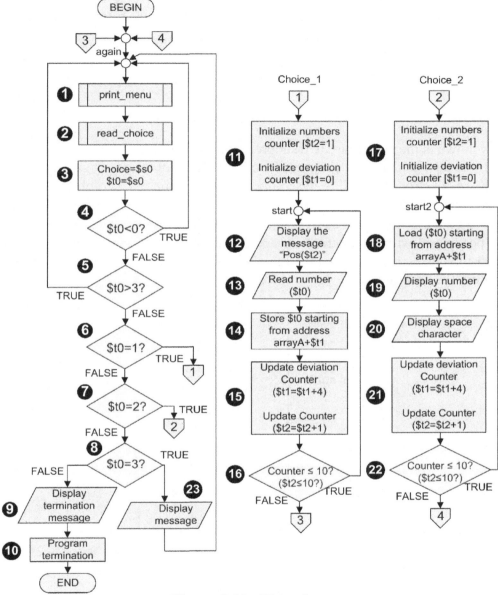

Figure 3.19a Flow chart

Figure 3.19b Flow chart

As shown in the flow chart, two subprograms are called and the execution flow returns later to the main program. The logic of subprograms is similar to the known functions. In MIPS Assembly, the instruction `jal` combined with a label, drives the execution flow to a specific point, while the register `$31` (i.e. `$ra`) contains the return address to the next of the call instruction. This return is performed with the instruction `jr $31`. Figure 3.20 shows the operation and the corresponding usage of the above instructions. The `sub1` is a label within the program.

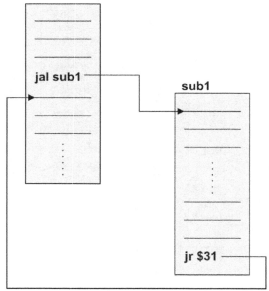

Figure 3.20 Subprogram call and return

The code development is as follows:

```
.text 0x00400000
```

again:

```
        jal print_menu
```

Call the subprogram `print_menu` for displaying the selection menu. The return is performed in the next instruction through the `jr $31` which exists within the subprogram `print_menu`.

```
        jal read_choice
```

Call the subprogram `read_choice` for reading the user selection. After the return to the next instruction, the register $s0 contains the user selection.

```
        move $t0,$s0
```

Load the user selection ($s0) in $t0.

```
        bltz $t0,again
```

If the user enters a selection (number) less than zero (not acceptable value), then the execution flow returns to `again` (program start) in order to display again the selection menu.

```
        bgt $t0,3,again
```

If the user enters a selection (number) greater than three (acceptable values 1,2,3 or 0), then the execution flow returns to again (program start) in order to display again the selection menu.

```
beq $t0,1,choice_1
```

If the first selection (fill array) has been chosen by the user, then the execution flow is driven to the section regarding the array fill.

```
beq $t0,2,choice_2
```

If the second selection (display array) has been chosen by the user, then the execution flow is driven to the section regarding the array display

```
beq $t0,3,choice_3
```

If the third selection has been chosen by the user (test selection), then the program just displays a message. This section can be populated by the programmer.

```
exodos:
```

```
li $v0,4
la $a0,exit_mes
syscall
```

For reaching that point, the user has chosen 0 (exit).

```
li $v0,10
syscall
```

Program termination with function 10

```
choice_1:
```

```
li $t2,1
```

If the first selection has been chosen by the user, then the array filling operation is activated. The counter ($t2) is initialized with 1 for counting how many number will be stored in array (from keyboard).

```
li $t1,0
```

Initialize deviation counter

```
start:
```

```
li $v0,4
la $a0,m1
syscall

li $v0,1
move $a0,$t2
syscall

li $v0,4
```

```
la $a0,m2
syscall
```

Before entering the number (keyboard), a message in the form "Pos[$t2]=" is displayed for informing user for the current array location

```
li $v0,5
syscall
move $t0,$v0
```

Read an integer number from the keyboard (store in $t0)

```
sw $t0,arrayA($t1)
```

The previous number ($t0) is stored in array starting from the address arrayA+$t1.

```
add $t1,$t1,4
```

Update deviation counter

```
add $t2,$t2,1
```

Update numbers counter (loop counter)

```
ble $t2,10,start
```

If all the numbers have not been read, then return to loop

```
    j again
```

Return to program start (display menu, etc, κλπ).

```
choice_2:
```

```
li $t2,1
```

Initialize counter for displaying array contents

```
li $t1,0
```

Initialize deviation counter

```
start2:
```

```
    lw $t0,arrayA($t1)
```

Read from array starting from the address arrayA+$t1 (store in $t0)

```
    li $v0,1
    move $a0,$t0
    syscall
```

Display array element ($t0)

```
li $v0,4
la $a0,spacechar
syscall
```

Display a space character (for reading more easily the console)

```
add $t1,$t1,4
```

Update deviation counter

```
add $t2,$t2,1
```

Update numbers counter (loop counter)

22

```
ble $t2,10,start2
```

If all the numbers have not been read, proceed to the next number

```
j again
```

Return to the program start (display menu, etc)

```
epilogi_3:
```

23

```
li $v0,4
la $a0,ep3
syscall
j again
```

Display a help message

```
print_menu:
```

```
    li $v0,4
    la $a0,menu
    syscall
    jr $31
```

Display menu and return to main program (through register $31)

```
read_choice:
```

```
    li $v0,5
    syscall
    move $s0,$v0
    jr $31
```

Read the user selection and return to main program (through register $31)

The complete code is following.

#Application 17
```
.text 0x00400000          #Code section
again:

    jal print_menu        #Call subprogram
                          #for displaying menu
    jal read_choice       #Call subprogram for
                          #reading the user's choice

    move $t0,$s0          #Store selection in $t0
    bltz $t0,again        #If selection <0, go to start
    bgt $t0,3,again       #If selection >3, go to start

    beq $t0,1,choice_1    #First selection: fill array
    beq $t0,2,choice_2    #Second selection: display array
    beq $t0,3,choice_3    #Third selection: for test only
```

```
exodos:
                                #Display the message
                                #"\n\nProgram termination"
        li $v0,4                 #Load the function number
        la $a0,exit_mes          #Load the message starting address
        syscall                  #Function call


                                 #Program termination
        li $v0,10                #Load the function number
        syscall                  #Function call

choice_1:                        #Fill array

li $t2,1                         #Loop counter
li $t1,0                         #Deviation counter

start:
                                 #Display the message "Pos["
        li $v0,4                 #Load the function number
        la $a0,m1                #Load the message starting address
        syscall                  #Function call


                                 #Display current array location
        li $v0,1                 #Load the function number
        move $a0,$t2             #Load the number to be displayed
        syscall                  #Function call


                                 #Display the message "]="
        li $v0,4                 #Load the function number
        la $a0,m2                #Load the message starting address
        syscall                  #Function call


                                 #Read number (keyboard)
        li $v0,5                 #Load the function number
        syscall                  #Function call
        move $t0,$v0             #Load the number in $t0


        sw $t0,arrayA($t1)      #Store the number in array starting
                                 #from the address arrayA+$t1
```

```
        add $t1,$t1,4           #Update deviation counter
        add $t2,$t2,1           #Update loop counter

        ble $t2,10,start        #If all the numbers have
                                #not been stored, go to start

        j again                 #Return to selection menu

choice_2:                       #Display array

li $t2,1                        #Numbers counter
li $t1,0                        #Deviation counter

start2:

        lw $t0,arrayA($t1)      #Read number from array

                                #Display number
        li $v0,1                #Load the function number
        move $a0,$t0            #Load the number to be displayed
        syscall                 #Function call

                                #Display a space character
        li $v0,4                #Load the function number
        la $a0,spacechar        #Load the message starting address
        syscall                 #Function call

        add $t1,$t1,4           #Update deviation counter
        add $t2,$t2,1           #Update loop counter

        ble $t2,10,start2       #If all the numbers
                                #have not been read, go to start2

        j again                 #Return to selection menu

choice_3:
                                #Display the message "\n C selected"
        li $v0,4                #Load the function number
```

```
        la $a0,ep3              #Load the message starting address
        syscall                 #Function call
        j again                 #Return to selection menu


print_menu:                     #Display selection menu


        li $v0,4                #Load the function number
        la $a0,menu             #Load the message starting address
        syscall                 #Function call
        jr $31                  #Return


read_choice:                    #Read menu selection


        li $v0,5                #Load the function number
        syscall                 #Function call
        move $s0,$v0            #Store selection in $s0
        jr $31                  #Return


                                #Data section
.data
menu:
        .ascii  "\n**********************"
        .ascii  "\n* 1. Fill array       *"
        .ascii  "\n* 2. Display array    *"
        .ascii  "\n* 3. Selection C      *"
        .ascii  "\n* 0. Exit             *"
        .ascii  "\n**********************"
        .asciiz "\nSELECT (1-3 or 0):"

ep3:        .asciiz "\n C selected"
exit_mes:   .asciiz "\n\nProgram trmination"
m1:         .asciiz "Pos["
m2:         .asciiz "]="
.align 2

arrayA: .space 40
spacechar: .asciiz " "
```

Figure 3.21 shows the selection menu.

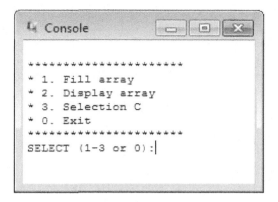

Figure 3.21 Selection menu

Figure 3.22 shows the array filling operation.

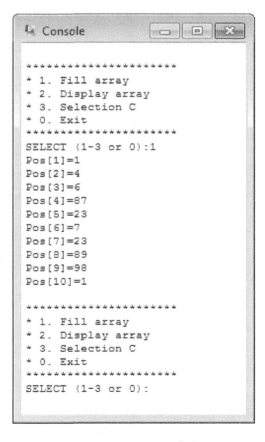

Figure 3.22 Array filling

4 Lab exercises

Content-Goals
In this chapter lab exercises organized in steps will be presented. This exercises are well structured for helping the students to work autonomously and to learn how to think.

Chapter contents

Introduction

The lab exercises within a course play a crucial role due to the fact that give to students the opportunity to develop and make experiments with programs. The coding experiments (structures, instructions, Assembly features) will give to the student a real picture for understanding in depth the microprocessor programming in Assembly language. Moreover, the main point is in the development methodology and how the student has to think. For the above reasons, the lab exercises are tightly structured in steps for helping the student to work effectively.

Exercise 1

Developing and executing programs in the simulator environment (SPIM)

Step 1

Initially, a simple text editor will be used for developing the source code (Assembly code). It is important to save the file without any format with the extension .s or .txt. In windows, the notepad is the most popular simple text editor.

In Linux, the text editor gedit or vi can be used.

Initially, enter the following source code (in the notepad for example):

```
.text 0x00400000

        li $v0,4
        la $a0,msg
        syscall

        li $v0,10
        syscall

.data
msg:
        .asciiz     "My first program"
```

Important: In the case of PCSPIM (older version of QtSpim), the label **main** have to be added before the directive .text.

Step 2

Next, the file will be saved with the extension .s. The save filter has to be used correctly in order to prevent adding and a second extension (select "All files" in the save window). In an incorrect save procedure, the file extension can be .s.txt.

Step 3

Now, the simulator has to be activated (SPIM/QtSPIM for Windows or xSPIM/QtSPIM for Linux). From the main menu, load the program (Load selection). The Assembly instructions are shown now within the text window.

Step 4

Execute the program by selecting *Simulator* → *Run* from the main menu. Observe the result on the console window (the console window can be activated from the menu *windows*).

Step 5

After the program execution, write the content of the register $v0 (Registers are shown in the IntRegs window of the simulator).

$v0=...........

Make comments regarding the content of $v0

Step 6

Find the Assembly instructions of your program within the simulator. Why there is a second column with other Assembly instructions?

Step 7
Write the initial address of the Assembly instructions of your program (first to third instruction).

Step 8
With which step the above addresses are changing (and why)?

Step 9
Based on step 8, write how many bytes constitute every instruction

Step 10
What does it mean the constant instruction length? Can you compare this system with other systems which use variable instruction length?

Step 11

The Data section contains the message `'My first program'`. Find that message within the simulator environment as well as the corresponding bytes. Compare the message bytes with the ASCII codes. Write the arithmetic code for every message symbol.

M	y	space	f	i	r	s	t	space	p	r	o	g	r	a	m

Step 12

How many bytes will constitute every message symbol if the symbols belongs to the Unicode set?

Step 13

Replace instruction `li $v0,4` with `LI $v0,4` in your first program. Save the new version and try to execute the program within the simulator. Read the error message and find out if it is understandable for correcting the error in source code.

Write the above error message that is displayed within the simulator.

Exercise 2

Using basic system functions

Step 1

Fill in the following box the result that is produced or the corresponding operation after the instruction execution of each code section. Read previous chapters for finding relevant information.

Code	Result-Operation
`.text 0x00400000`	

`#Section 1`
`li $v0,4`
`la $a0,msg1`
`syscall`	

`#Section 2`
`li $v0,5`
`syscall`
`move $t0,$v0`	

`#Section 3`
`li $v0,4`
`la $a0,msg2`
`syscall`	

`#Section 4`
`li $v0,1`
`move $a0,$t0`
`syscall`	

`#Section 5`
`li $v0,10`
`syscall`	

`.data`
`msg1: .asciiz "Enter`
`number:"`
`msg2: .asciiz "The number`
`is:"`	

Step 2

Why the instruction `move $t0,$v0` is used after reading the integer number from the keyboard?

Step 3

Test the code of step 1 in the simulator and observe the corresponding results in the console window.

Step 4

What changes have to be done in the code of step 1 in order to read three numbers in total?

Step 5

Is it possible to avoid the help messages during the numbers read?

YES		NO	

Step 6

For reading three numbers and displaying a help message for every number, how many times the functions 4 and 5 have to be called? With which sequence?

Number of calls (function 4)	
Number of calls (function 5)	

Call sequance

Step 7

Develop and test in the simulator, the corresponding program of step 4 without displaying help message during the numbers input. Make comments.

Step 8
Find the addition instruction for adding two numbers that are stored in registers.

Instruction for addition	

Step 9
Use the addition instruction for adding the first and the second number (use the program of step 7). Next, display the result on the screen using the help message '(X+Y) ='.

Step 10
Write in the following box the new code for adding and displaying result based on the previous step.

Instruction for adding the two numbers	
Instructions for displaying the message '(X+Y) ='	
Instructions for displaying result	

Exercise 3

Implementing more complex arithmetic calculations

Step 1
The program that will be developed, calculates the difference A-B-C (where A,B,C are integer numbers that are entered from the keyboard). If the three numbers are stored in the registers $t1, $t2 and $t3 respectively, write in the following box the needed instructions for calculating $t1-$t2-$t3 (i.e. A-B-C).

Instructions for calculating A-B-C (A=$t1, B=$t2, C=$t3)	

As will be shown next, the arithmetic calculation will be displayed in a parameterized form. If for example the numbers 3,1 and 1 are entered, then the result will be displayed in the form $(3-1-1)=1$.

Due to the fact that integer numbers and messages are displayed using different functions, write in the following box how many and what functions are needed for displaying the above result.

Function number:	Number of calls	Function number:	Number of calls ....

Step 2

Develop on your notepad, a program for calculating the difference of three numbers (A-B-C) and displaying the corresponding result.

Step 3

Write in the following box, the needed code section for displaying the above result in the parameterized form (assume that A=3, B=1, C=1).

Code	Result on screen

Step 4
Write the contents of the data section that are used for displaying the result in the parameterized form.

```
.data

```

Step 5
Test the previous program in the simulator.

Step 6
If A=$t1, B=$t2 and C=$t3, write in the next box the needed code for implementing the following calculations:

Calculation	Code
Z1=(A/B)+C	
Z2=A+2*(C/B)	
Z3=A*B*C	
Z4=C/(B-A)	

Step 7

Develop and test the program that implements step 6 and displays the corresponding results in the following form:

Z1=first arithmetic result
Z2=second arithmetic result
Z3=third arithmetic result
Z4=fourth arithmetic result

Step 8

Which modifications have to be made for displaying Z1 in parameterized form?

Step 9

Develop and test a complete program for displaying Z1, Z2, Z3 and Z4 in the parameterized form.

Exercise 4

Condition-check with branch instructions (A)

Step 1

Analyze the operation of the following program and sketch the corresponding flow chart by studying the MIPS instructions.

Code	Flow chart
`bgt $t1,10,cont` `li $v0,4`	

```
la $a0,msg1
syscall

j exit

cont:
li $v0,4
la $a0,msg2
syscall

exit:

li $v0,10
syscall

.data
msg1: .asciiz
"message 1"
msg2:.asciiz
"message 2"
```

Step 2

In which cases the messages 'message 1' and 'message 2' are displayed?

'message 1'	
'message 2'	

Step 3

The following program displays a message if the content of a register belongs to a value range. More precisely, the number is checked if belongs to the value range [10,20]. Write in the next box the corresponding pseudocode or C code.

Code	Pseudocode or C code
blt $t1,10,exit bgt $t1,20,exit li $v0,4	

```
la $a0,msg
syscall

exit:

li $v0,10
syscall

.data

msg: .asciiz "$t1 belongs to
[10,20]"
```

Step 4
An alternative way of check, is to investigate if the number is greater or equal to the left limit. If this is TRUE, then it is checked if the number is less or equal to the right limit. If both condition-checks are TRUE, then the number belongs to that value range.
Write in next box the corresponding pdeudocode which represents that logic.

Step 5
Develop and test the corresponding program for step 4.

Step 6
Search for the most suitable instructions in order to implement in Assembly the corresponding code for a do-while structure. Study the following indicative C code.

C code	Assembly code
x=1	....
do	....
{	

printf("my message");
 	
x++;
 	
}
while (x<=10)
	#Display message
	
	....
	
	....

Step 7
Write in your notepad the corresponding pseudocode or C code for implementing the structure while-do.

Step 8
Develop in Assembly the program of step 7.

Step 9
Develop and test an Assembly program for an iteration loop which displays your name 15 times based on step 6.

Step 10
Develop and test an Assembly program for an iteration loop which displays your name 15 times based on step 7.

Exercise 5
Condition-check with branch instructions (B)

Step 1
The following program is given:

```
      li $t0,0
      li $t1,1
start:
      mul $t2,$t1,$t1
      add $t0,$t0,$t2
      add $t1,$t1,1
      ble $t1,10,start
```

Write in the following box what calculation is performed by the above program

[blank box]

Step 2

Write the corresponding pseudocode or C code for the program of step 1.

[blank box]

Step 3

In this step, a program which reads three numbers and performs some calculations will be developed. The program performs some calculations based on the following conditions:

If (A+B) >0,   calculation of A*(3+C)
If (A+B)=0,   calculation of C-(3C+5A)
If (A+B)<0,   calculation of A+B-C^2

If the calculation A+B is initially performed, how many checks have to be implemented for the three above cases?

Number of checks	

If the above calculations are implemented in code sections that start from the labels `megcode`, `isocode` and `mikcode` respectively, write in the following box the needed condition-checks with branching to the correct code sections.

[blank box]

```


```

Step 4
Develop and test the Assembly program for step 3.

Step 5
Using the knowledge from the program of the previous step, develop new code for performing calculations under condition as follows:

If (A+B-C)<0, calculation of $1^3+2^3+...+10^3$

If (A+B-C)>5, and (A+B-C) belongs to [6,10], then calculate $10^2+9^2+...+1^2$

If (A+B-C)=5, display the message HELLO

How many condition-checks are needed for the (A+B-C)?

Number of checks	

Step 6
Test the program of step 5 in the simulator.

Exercise 6

Condition-check with branch instructions (C)

Step 1
For finding the roots of a trinomial, the calculation $\Delta=\beta^2-4\alpha\gamma$ has to be made, where α,β and γ are the corresponding coefficients.

Fill in the boxes the needed instructions for the following calculations (assume that $1=\alpha$, $t2=\beta$ and $t3=\gamma$):

$\alpha\gamma$	
$4\alpha\gamma$	

β^2	
$\beta^2-4\alpha\gamma$	

Develop in your notepad an Assembly program for reading the coefficients α,β and γ, calculating Δ and displaying messages based on the Δ value.

Δ=0   message a double root
Δ>0   message two real roots
Δ<0   message imaginary roots

Step 2
Write in the boxes the needed instructions for the following calculations:

Calculation 1 (example) $f(x) = \dfrac{x^2 - x}{x + 2}$	Calculation 2 (example) x mod 2

Code for calculation 1
 	
Assume that $t1=x
 	
`mul $t2,$t1,$t1  #x²`
`sub $t2,$t2,$t1  #x²-x`
`add $t3,$t1,2    #x+2`
`div $t3,$t2,$t3  #f(x)`
	Code for calculation 2
	
	Assume that $t1=x
	
	`li $t2,2`
	`div $t1,$t2`
	`mfhi $t2 #$t2=integer`
	`remainder`

Calculation 3 $f(x) = \dfrac{(x - 2)mod2}{x^3 - 1}$	**Calculation 4** $f(x) = \dfrac{x^3 mod x}{2(x^2 mod2)}$
Code for calculation 3	**Code for calculation 4**

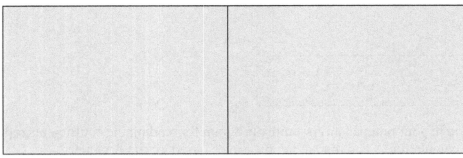

Calculation 5
$$f(x) = x^2 + x^3 - \frac{1}{(x-3)(x+1)}$$
Code for calculation 5

Use the instruction div (not rem) with two arguments and the instruction mfhi for processing the remainder

Step 3
Develop and test in the simulator the needed programs regarding the above calculations.

Step 4
Modify the program of step 3 in order not to allow numbers that makes zero the denominator (defensive programming). Initially the X will be entered and only the denominator will be calculated as a second step. If the result is not zero, then the whole calculation (f(x)) will be performed.

Exercise 7
Condition-check and iteration loops

Step 1
One of the most known methods to convert integer numbers from decimal to binary is the successive divisions. The divisions are made with the binary system base. Write in the box the needed divisions for converting the number 78 from the decimal to binary system.

Step 2
Which are the conditions for terminating the successive divisions?

With which sequence the division remainders are read?

[ ]

Which remainder represents the most significant digit?

[ ]

Which numbers are successivelly divided by 2?

[ ]

Step 3

Write in the box the corresponding pseudocode or C code for the successive divisions.

[ ]

Note: Due to the fact that no arrays are used, the remainder is displayed in the order that is produced. Thus, the exercise is not fully completed (a digits sequence inversion is needed). In some computer systems the above inversion is not needed because the produced numbers can be read in the opposite direction (the MSB is on the right).

Step 4

Develop in Assembly code the needed conversion. Use the instruction `div` with two arguments.

Step 5

Test the program operation within the simulator environment.

Step 6

Develop a pseudocode for displaying asterisks as follows:

```
*
**
***
****
*****
```

For developing the corresponding code, look carefully the above shape. The most important observation in the above shape is that the number of asterisks is based on the line number. For example, the first line has one asterisk, the second line has two asterisks, and so on. Assuming that the number of line is N, then an iteration loop from A=1 to N has to be developed, while for every line B=1 to A asterisks have to be displayed.

Step 7
Develop the corresponding program on your notepad and then test the operation in the simulator. The maximum number of asterisks-lines is entered from the keyboard.

Exercise 8
Introduction to arrays

Step 1
All the data that are processed by the programs are hosted in the main memory of the computer. It is already known that the memory is an one dimensional array. That means that every time a programmer declares a two dimensional array, the corresponding data are finally stored in an one dimensional array (memory). Assuming that a programmer has created an array 2 x 4 (the following array), write in the following boxes the contents of the corresponding one dimensional array in the memory starting from the address DFA0.

2	67	21	98

5	10	233	4

Address	Content
DFA0	

Step 2

Due to the fact that in classic memory models every location hosts 1 byte, how many memory locations are needed for storing the numbers 12, 256, 1356, 24512, 32766;

Number	Number of memory locations
12	
256	
1356	
24512	
32766	

Step 3

Which is the value range (unsigned numbers) that can be hosted in two memory locations?

Step 4

How many memory locations are needed for storing the content of four general purpose registers of the MIPS microprocessor?

Step 5

In an Assembly program, a logical array of 4 rows (hosting a register in each logical row) has been declared starting from the address `pinA`. Write the starting addresses for every stored register (starting from the address F000). Write also the relative addresses (based on the label `pinA`) of the array (logical array) where each stored register starts.

	Absolute address	Symbolic address (relative)
Starting address first register		
Starting address second register		
Starting address third register		
Starting address fourth register		

Step 6

Sketch the logical and the physical array that hosts 5 registers in total.

Step 7

Assume the bytes Kx_2, Kx_1, Kx_0 of register x. Starting from the address AFF0 write the corresponding bytes for storing three registers.

Register byte	Address	Register
Kl_2	AFF0	
Kl_1		First
Kl_0		
		Second
		Third

Step 8

The following program fills a logical array of 5 rows. Write the missing instructions.

```
li $t2,1
      . . . . . . . . . . . . . . . . .
  start:
      li $v0,5
      syscall
      move $t0,$v0
      sw . . . . . . . . . . . . . . ,pinA(. . . . . . . . . . . . . . )
      . . . . . . . . . . . . . . . . .
      addi $t2,$t2,1
      ble $t2,5,start
.data

pinA: .space 20
```

Step 9

Develop the corresponding code for displaying the array contents.

Step 10
Develop a fully operational program in the simulator for filling and displaying an array of 10 rows (locations).

Step 11
Which modifications have to be made (program of step 8) in order to store only one byte of the register $t0?

Modification

Step 12
Write and analyze the differences that are produced by the instructions `lw`, `lb` and `lh`.

Step 13

Modify the program of step 10 for displaying a help message during the filling of the array. This message will be displayed for every number that is entered by the user. For example, the help message for the two first numbers will be:

```
A[0]=
A[1]=
```

Exercise 9

Array management (A)

Step 1

Write the needed code for calculating the square of a positive number. Assume that the number is stored in $t1.

Step 2

Develop a program for calculating the square of positive numbers of an array. The resulted square will be store in the same array location. The above operation can be described as follows:

```
A=array[i]
B=A*A
array[i]=B
```

Step 3

Write a program for calculating and displaying the summation of the numbers that are stored in an array.

Step 4

Write the code for checking a number if it is odd or even.

Step 5
Develop a program for displaying how many numbers are odd and the corresponding summation of the even numbers in an array.

Step 6
Develop a program for finding how many zero numbers exist only if the number of even numbers is greater than the number of odd numbers in an array.

Step 7
Assume an array of 10 logical rows (locations) starting from the address `PinA`. Write on your notepad the needed code in order to display the array contents in a reverse order.

Step 8
Use step 7 in order to complete the previous (not fully completed) exercise for converting a number from the decimal to the binary system.

Step 9
Modify the code of step 8 in order not to display the unnecessary zeros.

* Assume in the above programs an array of 10 rows (locations) that is filled from the keyboard

Exercise 10
Array management (B)

Step 1
Assuming two arrays `PinA` and `PinB`, write the code for swapping the contents of the two arrays. Use register $t1 as a deviation counter.

Step 2

Develop a complete Assembly program for swapping the contents of the arrays `PinA` and `PinB`. The arrays content before and after the swap operation have to be displayed.

Step 3

Write a program for swapping the first half with the second half of an array of 10 logical rows (locations). Connect with the correct arrows the corresponding array locations.

Step 4

Assume that in a logical array, the winter temperature measurements have been stored. Write a program for displaying the temperatures distribution using an histogram. For every temperature (array location) a corresponding number of asterisks has to be displayed. The results on screen will be displayed in the following form:

[0]**
[1]**********
[2]****
[3]******
and so on

For example, in the first array location (location 0) the temperature of 2 Celsius degrees has been stored, in the second location (location 1) the temperature of 10 Celsius degrees has been stored, and so on.

Step 5

Develop a program for displaying in an histogram form the diagram of the function $f(x)=x^2$. **Note:** for simplicity reasons, the diagram will be displayed with reversed axes. Thus, for every value of x, the f(x) will be calculated and the corresponding asterisks will be displayed. The value range will be -10 to 10.

Step 6
Modify the program of the step 5 in order to display only the surrounding of the diagram. Thus, if Y=f(x), then Y-1 spaces and one asterisk will be displayed.

Step 7
Develop a program for filling an array 3x3. The relation between two arrays of one and two dimensions has to be found. Write on your notepad the analysis of the above relation (make an example with symbolic addresses).

	0	1	2
0	0,0	0,1	0,2
1	1,0	1,1	1,2
2	2,0	2,1	2,2

Address	Content

Address = (row * ....) + ...

Step 8
If a 3x3 array starts from the symbolic address arrayA which corresponds to the physical address BF00, write on your notepad the symbolic (relevant) and physical addresses where the elements of the array diagonal begin.

Array element	Physical address	Symbolic address
(0,0)		
(1,1)		
(2,2)		

Step 9
Develop a complete program for displaying the elements of the main diagonal of a 3x3 array.

* Assume in the above programs an array of 10 rows (locations) that is filled from the keyboard

Exercise 11
Subprograms

Step 1
The following code is given:

Assembly code	C code
```start: jal read_choice move $t0,$s0 bltz $t0,start bgt $t0,3,start beq $t0,1,choice_1 beq $t0,2,choice_2 beq $t0,3,choice_3 beqz $t0,termination read_choice: .... jr ....#return termination:```	

Analyze the operation of the above Assembly code and develop the corresponding C code. Inside the C code use the proper void functions.

Step 2
Develop a fully operational program for implementing the logic of the step 1. Initially, place code only for display messages inside the subprograms `choice_1` to `choice_3`.

Step 3
Modify the program of step 2 in order to display a selection menu before reading the user selection. Use the following menu form:

```
===========
1. Item 1
2. Item 2
3. Item 3
0. Exit
===========
```

Step 4
Write a program for performing the basic four arithmetic operations between two numbers that entered from the keyboard. The operation selection will be done through a selection menu. Use the following structure for the selection menu:

```
================
1. Addition
2. Subtraction
3. Multiplication
4. Division
0. Exit
================
```

Every time an arithmetic operation is performed, the corresponding result will be displayed on the screen and the execution flow will be returned to the selection menu. The program will be terminated only when the user enters the selection zero.

Step 5
Write a program for simulating the stack operation. The selection menu includes the following items:

```
================
1. Initialization
2. Push
3. Pop
0. Exit
================
```

The stack status after each selection activation has to be displayed as follows:

```
|*
|*
|45 <== SP
|3
|233
|5
==
```

Where SP is the Stack Pointer and * an available position (location) in the stack.

Exercise 12
Subprograms and arrays

Step 1
In previous exercises, programs for arrays management have been developed (filling, displaying, arithmetic operations, etc). Develop a program for managing a logical array of 10 rows using the following selection menu:

```
==================
1. Fill array
2. Display array
0. Exit
==================
```

After the filling or displaying operation, the execution flow returns to the selection menu and will be terminated only if the user activates the selection 0.

Step 2
Write the algorithm for finding the minimum and the maximum value inside an array.

Finding the minimum value	Finding the maximum value

Step 3

Develop a complete program for finding and displaying the minimum and the maximum number in an array. Use the following menu form:

```
================
1. Fill array
2. Display array
3. Find minimum
4. Find maximum
0. Exit
================
```

The program is terminated only if the selection 0 is activated.

Step 4

Populate the program of step 3 for implementing new operations as follows:

- Sum
- Display zero positive and negative numbers
- Sorting

Exercise 13

String manipulation

Step 1

Use the following program for reading a string from the keyboard.

```
.text 0x00400000

    li $v0,8
    la $a0,alpha
    li $a1,11
    syscall
```

```
        li $v0,10
        syscall
.data
alpha:  .space 11
```

Step 2

Modify the program of step 1 in order to display the string on the screen using the function 4.

Step 3

Write the bytes that represent the string that has been entered from the keyboard (search in the text area of the simulator)

Step 4

It is known that in the ASCII code the symbols ['a','z'] have a constant distance from the symbols ['A','Z'] (symbol by symbol). For example, the symbols 'a' and 'A' have the same distance as well as the symbols 'f' and 'F'. Develop the algorithm for converting the small letters to capitals in a word that is stored in an array.

Step 5

Develop a fully operational program for implementing the algorithm of step 4.

Step 6

Develop a program that encrypts a phrase up to 20 characters by replacing each symbol with the next one.

Step 7
Write a program for implementing the decryption based on step 6.

Step 8
Write a program for displaying the occurrence frequency of the symbol 'a' in a phrase up to 20 characters.

Step 9
Develop a program for displaying in an histogram the occurrence frequency of the characters 'a' and 'b' in a phrase up to 30 characters.

5 Selected MIPS Assembly Instructions

Content-Goals
In this chapter, the basic MIPS Assembly instructions will be presented as well as instruction lists with the corresponding description.

Instructions and functions of the MIPS Assembly

add

Operation

Add the content of two registers or add a register with an integer value

Expression

```
add r1,r2,ri
```

r1,r2 = register (register name)
ri = register (register name) or integer value

Description

r1 = r2 + ri

Example

#Adding registers
```
add $t0,$t1,$t2 #$t0=$t1+$t2
```

#Adding a register and an integer value
```
add $t0,$t1,4 #$t0=$t1+4
```

#Implementing the addition $t0=$t1+$t2+$t3
```
add $t0,$t1,$t2
add $t0,$t0,$t3
```

This instruction works as a pseudoinstruction when the third argument is an integer value. In such a case, the real instruction is `addi` (the `add` instruction is automatically converted to `addi` by the system).

sub

Operation

Subtract the content of two registers or subtract an integer value from a register

Expression

```
sub r1,r2,ri
```

r1,r2 = register (register name)
ri = register (register name) or integer value

Description

r1 = r2 - ri

Example

#Subtracting registers
```
sub $t0,$t1,$t2 #$t0=$t1-$t2
```

#Subtracting an integer value from a register
```
sub $t0,$t1,4 #$t0=$t1-4
```

#Implementing the subtraction $t0=$t1-$t2-$t3
```
sub $t0,$t1,$t2
sub $t0,$t0,$t3
```

mul

Operation

Multiply two registers or multiply a register with an integer value

Expression

```
mul r1,r2,ri
```

r1,r2 = register (register name)
ri = register (register name) or integer value

Description

r1 = r2 * ri

Example

#Multiplying registers
```
mul $t0,$t1,$t2 #$t0=$t1*$t2
```

#Multiplying an integer value with a register
```
mul $t0,$t1,4 #$t0=$t1*4
```

#Implementing the multiplication $t0=$t1*$t2*$t3
```
mul $t0,$t1,$t2
mul $t0,$t0,$t3
```

div (three arguments)

Operation

Divide two registers or divide a register with an integer value

Expression

```
div r1,r2,ri
```

r1,r2 = register (register name)
ri = register (register name) or integer value

Description

r1 = r2 / ri

Example

#Dividing registers
```
div $t0,$t1,$t2 #$t0=$t1/$t2
```

#Dividing a register with an integer value
```
div $t0,$t1,4 #$t0=$t1/4
```

Note

Due to the fact that the corresponding arithmetic operations are based on the integer arithmetic, any fractional part is rejected and only the integer part is kept without any rounding operation. If for example the result is 0.7, then the result inside the register is 0.

div (two arguments)

Operation

Divide two registers and store the result automatically in other registers.

Expression

```
div r1,r2
```

r1,r2 = register (register name)

Description

HI=Remainder (r1/r2), LO=Quotient (r1/r2)

Example

#Dividing with an integer value
```
li $t2,2    #Load the integer value
div $t1,$t2
```

Note

Due to fact that the registers HI and LO are special registers they cannot be used directly in the program. For using HI and LO, the corresponding content has to be copied to general purpose registers. Instructions mfhi and mflo implements the needed transfer respectively (example mfhi $t3 #$t3=[HI]).

li

Operation

Load an integer value to a register

Expression

```
li r,v
```

r = register (register name)
v = integer value

Description

r = v

Example

#Loading a positive value
```
li $v0,1            #v0=1
```

#Loading a negative value
```
li $t1,-1           #v0=-1
```

#Usage in a function call
```
li $v0,4
la $a0,msg
syscall

.data
msg: .asciiz "Hello"
```

In the above example, the instruction li $v0,4 is used for defining which function will be called through the syscall.

#Wrong usage
```
li $t1,$t2          #A different instruction has to be used for loading
                    #data from register to register
```

move

Operation

Load the content of a register to another register

Expression

```
move r1,r2
```

r1 = destination register (register name)
r2 = source register (register name)

Description

r1 = r2

Example

#Loading
```
move $t1,$v0                    #$t1=$v0
```

#Usage in a function call
```
li $v0,1
move $a0,$t1
syscall
```

In the above example, the instruction move $a0,$t1 is used for moving the content of $t1 in $a0 in order to display the content of $t1 through the function 1.

la

Operation

Load an address in a register

Expression

```
la r, label
```

r = register (register name)
label = symbolic address (label)

Description

The real address that is represented by the label label is loaded in register r. Labels constitute useful tools for the programmer in order to define reference points inside the code. When the program is under execution, the symbolic addresses (labels) are automatically converted in real addresses (through the instruction la).

Example

#Loading an address
```
la $t1, panayotis        #$t1=address represented by panayotis
```

#Usage in a function call
```
li $v0,4
la $a0,panayotis
syscall

.data
panayotis: .asciiz "Hello"
```

In the above example, the instruction la $a0,panayotis is used for informing the function where the string starts (message).

lb

Operation

Load one byte from memory to a register

Expression

```
lb  r, addr
```

r = register (register name)
addr = memory address (symbolic or absolute)

Description

The content (1 byte) of the memory location addr is loaded in register r. The address definition can be done using a label combined with a register or directly through a hexadecimal number. In the first case, the register content is added with the corresponding address of the label in order to determine the real memory location.

Example

#Loading a byte directly from an address
```
lb $t1, 0x10000000      #$t1=[0x10000000]
```

#Usage in an array
```
lb $t1,arrayA($s0)

.data
arrayA: .space 10
```

In the above example, the instruction lb $t1,arrayA($s0) loads a byte which is stored in the address arrayA+($s0). Thus, if the label arrayA corresponds to the array starting address, then the register $s0 is used as a deviation from that location.

lh

Operation

Load two bytes (half word) from memory to a register

Expression

```
lh  r,  addr
```

r = register (register name)
addr = memory address (symbolic or absolute)

Description

The content of two successive memory locations (2 bytes) starting from the address `addr` are loaded in the register `r`. The address can be defined using a label combined with a register or using directly a hexadecimal number.

Example

#Loading directly two bytes from an address
#using a hexadecimal number
```
lh $t1, 0x10000000      #$t1=[0x10000000], [0x10000001]
```

#Reading from an array
```
lh $t1,arrayA($s0)
```

```
.data
arrayA: .space 10
```

In the above example the instruction `lh $t1,arrayA($s0)` loads two bytes starting from the address arrayA+($s0). Thus, the label `arrayA` corresponds to the initial array address and the data are loaded from the addresses arrayA+($s0) and arrayA+($s0)+1 respectivelly.

lw

Operation

Load four bytes (word) from memory to a register

Expression

```
lw r, addr
```

r = register (register name)
addr = memory address (symbolic or absolute)

Description

The content of four successive memory locations (4 bytes) starting from the address `addr` are loaded in the register `r`. The address can be defined using a label combined with a register or using directly a hexadecimal number.

Example

#Loading directly four bytes from an address
#using a hexadecimal number
```
lw $t1, 0x10000000 # 0x10000000 to 0x10000003
```

#Reading from an array
```
lw $t1,arrayA($s0)

.data
arrayA: .space 10
```

In the above example the instruction `lw $t1,arrayA($s0)` loads four bytes starting from the address arrayA+($s0). Thus, if the label `arrayA` corresponds to the initial array address, then the data are loaded from the addresses arrayA+($s0), arrayA+($s0)+1, arrayA+($s0)+2, and arrayA+($s0)+3 respectively.

SW

Operation

Store four bytes (word) from a register to memory

Expression

```
sw r, addr
```

r = register (register name)
addr = memory address (symbolic or absolute)

Description

The whole content of the register r is stored in memory starting from the address addr. The address can be defined using a label combined with a register or using directly a hexadecimal number.

Example

#Storing a register in memory
```
sw $t1, 0x10000000      #initial address
```

#Filling an array
```
sw $t1,arrayA($s0)

.data
arrayA: .space 10
```

In the above example the instruction sw $t1,arrayA($s0) stores the content of the $t1 in memory starting from the address arrayA+($s0). Thus, if the label arrayA corresponds to the initial array address, then the data are stored in the memory locations arrayA+($s0), arrayA+($s0)+1, arrayA+($s0)+2, and arrayA+($s0)+3 respectively.

Display an integer number (Function 1)

Operation

Display an integer number on screen

Requirements

The function number has to be loaded in the register $v0, while the number to be displayed has to be loaded in the register $a0.

Output

The number is displayed on screen

Expression (for function call)

```
li $v0,1
move $a0,r # $a0=destination register
syscall
```

r = register (register name)

Description

The above function displays on screen an integer number that is hosted in $a0. Based on the value source (register or integer value) the proper load instruction has to be used.

Examples

#Displaying the content of $t1
```
li $v0,1
move $a0,$t1
syscall
```

#Displaying the value 14
```
li $v0,1
li $a0,14
syscall
```

#Displaying the starting address of the message (string) with label mes1
```
li $v0,1
la $a0,mes1
syscall
```

Read an integer value (Function 5)

Operation

Read an integer number from keyboard

Requirements

The function number has to be loaded in $v0

Output

The entered number is automatically stored in the register $v0

Expression (for the function call)

```
li $v0,5
syscall
```

Description

The above function reads an integer number from the keyboard. This number is automatically stored in $v0. If the register $v0 is used just after the function call, then the entered number has to be temporarily stored in another register. The function call with the temporarily storage of the entered number will be implemented as follows:

```
li $v0,5
syscall
move $t1,$v0
```

Example

```
li $v0,5
syscall
move $t1,$v0

li $v0,5
syscall
move $t2,$v0
```

In the above example, two numbers are read from the keyboard and are temporarily stored in the registers $t1 and $t2 respectively.

Display a string (Function 4)

Operation

Display a message (string) on screen

Requirements

The function number has to be loaded in the register $v0, while the initial message address has to be loaded in the register $a0.

Output

Displays a message on screen

Expression (for function call)

```
li $v0,4
la $a0,mes1
syscall
```

Description

The above function displays the selected message on screen. The message has to be declared in the data section. During the program execution, the message label is converted to a real address.

Example

```
        li $v0,4
        la $a0,mes1
        syscall

        li $v0,4
        la $a0,mes2
        syscall
.data
mes1:  .asciiz "HELLO-1\n"
mes2:  .asciiz "HELLO-2"
```

The above example displays on the screen the messages HELLO-1 and HELLO-2 in different lines.

Read a string (Function 8)

Operation

Read a string from the keyboard

Requirements

The function number has to be loaded in the register $v0, the initial address where the string will begin to store has to be loaded in the register $a0 and the corresponding string length has to be stored in the register $a1 (together with the termination character).

Output

-

Expression (for function call)

```
        li $v0,8
        la $a0,abuffer
        li $a1,11
        syscall

.data
        abuffer: .space 11
```

The above program reads a string of length 10 from the keyboard (+1 for the termination character). The string is stored in a memory area which starts from the address `abuffer`.

Program termination (Function 10)

Operation

Terminate the program operation (exit)

Requirements

The function number has to be loaded in $v0.

Output

-

Expression (for function call)

```
li $v0,10
syscall
```

Instruction tables (synopsis)

Arithmetic instructions	
add Rdest, Rsrc1, Src2	Rdest = Rsrc1 + Src2
addi Rdest, Rsrc1, integer	Rdest = Rsrc1 + integer
div Rsrc1, Rsrc2	Rsrc1 / Rsrc2, HI=remainder, LO=quotient
div Rdest, Rsrc1, Src2	Rdest = Rsrc1 / Src2 (quotient)
mul Rdest, Rsrc1, Src2	Rdest = Rsrc1 * Src2
mult Rsrc1, Rsrc2	Rsrc1* Rsrc2, LO=low order word, HI=high order word
neg Rdest, Rsrc	Rdest = - Rsrc
rem Rdest, Rsrc1, Src2	Rdest = Rsrc1 / Src2 (remainder)
sub Rdest, Rsrc1, Src2	Rdest = Rsrc1 - Src2
Src2 = register or numerical value (16 bit integer).	
Rdest, Rsrc1, Rsrc2 = registers	

Constant manipulation	
li Rdest, integer	Rdest = integer

Comparison instructions

`seq Rdest, Rsrc1, Src2`	Rdest = 1 if Rsrc1 == Src2 and 0 in other case
`sge Rdest, Rsrc1, Src2`	Rdest = 1 if Rsrc1 >= Src2 and 0 in other case
`sgt Rdest, Rsrc1, Src2`	Rdest = 1 if Rsrc1 > Src2 and 0 in other case
`sle Rdest, Rsrc1, Src2`	Rdest = 1 if Rsrc1 <= Src2 and 0 in other case
`slt Rdest, Rsrc1, Src2`	Rdest = 1 if Rsrc1 < Src2 and 0 in other case
`slti Rdest, Rsrc1, integer`	Rdest = 1 if Rsrc1 < integer and 0 in other case
`sne Rdest, Rsrc1, Src2`	Rdest = 1 if Rsrc1 <> Src2 and 0 in other case
Src2 = register or numerical value (16 bit integer).	
Rdest, Rsrc1 = registers	

Branch-jump instructions

`b label`	branch to the instruction which starts at label (unconditional)
`beq Rsrc1, Src2, label`	branch to the instruction which starts at label if Rsrc1 = Src2
`beqz Rsrc, label`	branch to the instruction which starts at label if Rsrc = 0
`bge Rsrc1, Src2, label`	branch to the instruction which starts at label if Rsrc1 >= Src2
`bgez Rsrc, label`	branch to the instruction which starts at label if Rsrc >= 0
`bgt Rsrc1, Src2, label`	branch to the instruction which starts at label if Rsrc1 > Src2

bgtz Rsrc, label	branch to the instruction which starts at label if Rsrc > 0
ble Rsrc1, Src2, label	branch to the instruction which starts at label if Rsrc1 <= Src2
blez Rsrc, label	branch to the instruction which starts at label if Rsrc <= 0
blt Rsrc1, Src2, label	branch to the instruction which starts at label if Rsrc1 < Src2
bltz Rsrc, label	branch to the instruction which starts at label if Rsrc < 0
bne Rsrc1, Src2, label	branch to the instruction which starts at label if Rsrc1 <> Src2
bnez Rsrc, label	branch to the instruction which starts at label if Rsrc <> 0
j label	jump to the instruction which starts at label (unconditional)
jr Rsrc	Jump to the instruction which starts from the address that is defined from the content of Rsrc (unconditional) (jr $31 or jr $ra for returning from a subprogram that is called with the instruction jal label)
jal label	Jump to the instruction that starts at label (store the return address in the register $31 or $ra)
Src2=register or integer.	
Rdest, Rsrc1 = registers	

Load instructions	
la Rdest, address	Load an address in Rdest
lw Rdest, address	Load a word (32 bits) in Rdest starting from the address address

lh Rdest, address	Load a half-word (16 bits) in Rdest starting from the address address
lb Rdest, address	Load a byte (8 bits) in Rdest from the address address

Store instructions	
sw Rsrc, address	Store a word (32bits) from the content of Rsrc starting from the address address
sh Rsrc, address	Store a half-word (16bits) from the content of Rsrc starting from the address address
sb Rsrc, address	Store a byte (8bits) from the content of Rsrc to the address address

Data transfer (copy) instructions	
move Rdest, Rsrc	Copy the contents of Rsrc in Rdest
mfhi Rdest	Copy the contents of HI in register Rdest
mflo Rdest	Copy the contents of LO in register Rdest
mthi Rdest	Copy the contents of Rdest in register HI
mtlo Rdest	Copy the contents of Rdest in register LO

Functions

Function	Function number ($v0)	Arguments
print_int	1	$a0 = integer
print_string	4	$a0 = string (alphanumeric)
read_int	5	
read_string	8	$a0 = starting address of the storage area $a1 = string length
Exit (program termination)	10	

The function activation requires the execution of the instruction **syscall** after the arguments preparation.

Directives

Name	Description
.ascii str	Store a string in memory without the termination character (e.g. .ascii "Hello")
.asciiz str	Store a string in memory with the termination character
.byte b1, ..., bn	Store the successive n bytes in memory
.data	Set then Data area starting point
.space n	Reserve n bytes (data section)
.text	Set the code starting point (a starting address can be also defined optionally)

A Developing and executing MIPS programs

Content-Goals
This appendix presents a step by step guide for developing and finally executing MIPS programs in the simulator environment (Search on Google: Spim simulator download, for the free software).

Step 1 Open a text editor

Open a text editor (e.g. notepad in windows)

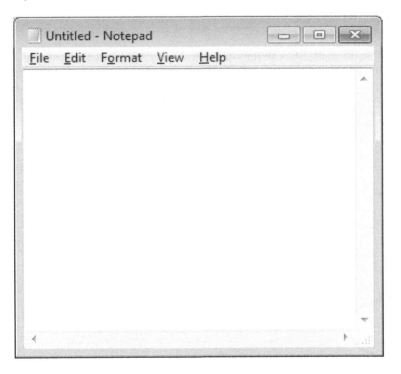

Step 2 Enter the source code

Enter the source code within the text editor

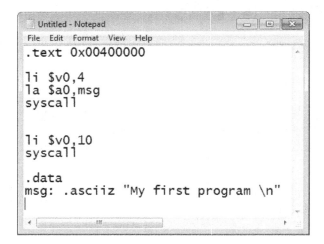

Step 3 Create source file

Save the source code in a file with the extension .s.

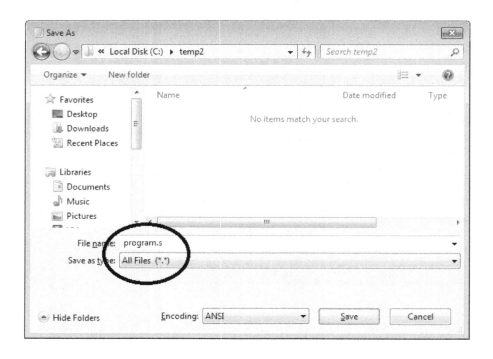

Step 4 Open file in simulator

Use the menu *File* (Load File) to open the source file.

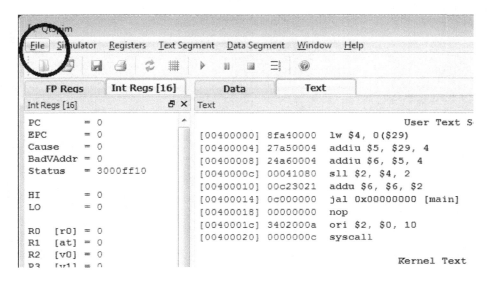

Step 5 Run the program

Execute the program by pressing the **play** button.

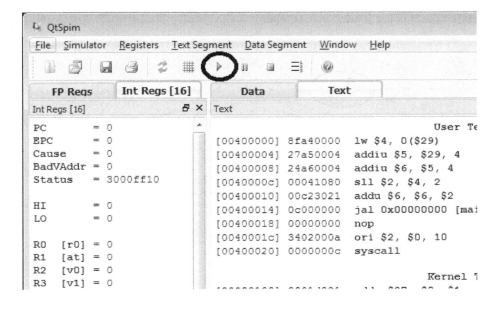

Step 6 Observe results

Observe the program results in the console window (use the selection *console* from the menu *window* if needed)

QtSpim Environment

Text section contains the loaded source code

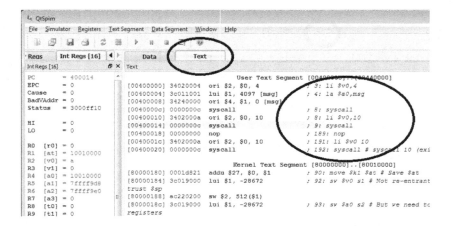

Data section contains the message

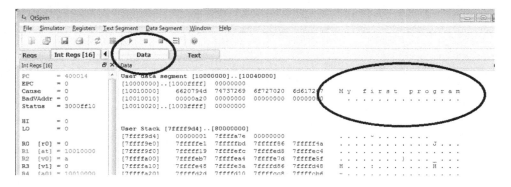

Int Regs section contains the MIPS integer registers

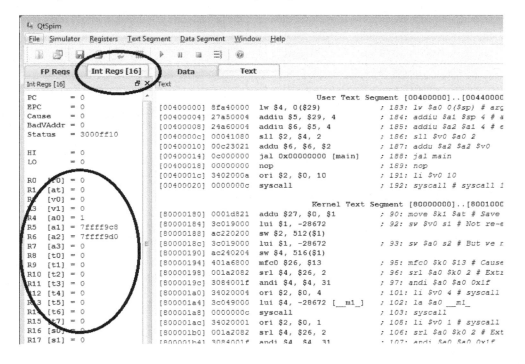

Made in the USA
Monee, IL
08 April 2022

94355882R00149